How to Analyze People

A Guide to Personality Types, Human Behavior, Dark Psychology, Emotional Intelligence, Persuasion, Manipulation, Speed-Reading People, Self-Awareness, and the Enneagram

Contents

Part 1: How to Analyze People

Unlocking the Secrets of Personality Types, Body Language, The Dark Psychology of Human Behavior, Emotional Intelligence, Persuasion, Manipulation, and Speed-Reading People

Chapter One: How We Connect

Throughout your life you have more than likely come upon a person who you simply couldn't figure out or understand. You felt this disconnect between the two of you—as if you simply existed in two separate worlds, planes that could never be joined together.

Maybe this took the form of someone you've met—a friend of a friend or an enigmatic colleague. Maybe it took the form of a character on your favorite show—their actions just screamed mysterious allure. Everything they did within the plot seemed to exist outside the realm of all the other characters and their ways of thinking. That character may have seemed on another level. We're drawn to these kinds of characters, both in the media and in the real world, if only because we want to understand what we can't seem to understand as humans—or as animals who want to know everything about everything, simply for the sake of knowledge. We can't help but watch them whenever we get the chance, just to try and understand them a little more. This is usually to no avail, however, but we still like to try every now and then.

Why do we love people-watching so much? This process, often referred to as naturalistic observation, is a practice often adopted by sociologists and behavioral psychologists, It's a way to view people in their "natural habitat"—that is to say, watching people interact without external stimulus that might alter how they would normally act in public.

Think of your favorite robot movie. Whether the robot is portrayed as a negative or positive force, there's likely some kind of sequence where they "learn" about humans—how they think, how they act, how they talk, and how they communicate with other humans. This is, in a sense, what other humans are doing when we sit down at a café or at a bench at the park and simply observe as people walk past us. As humans, we are deeply fascinated with ourselves as a species and as individuals. Therefore, to satisfy this fascination, we may find ourselves drawn to the monologues and the storylines of the random strangers we meet on the street. Chances are, you've had some strange and borderline cryptic encounter with a stranger on the street who was so incredibly fascinating in how different yet similar they were to you. You felt compelled to know more, if only out of some kind of macabre curiosity.

There are many answers to the question: "Why do we like to watch other people so much?" You would likely encounter a different answer from every person you to asked. Answers may include that it's mere curiosity or that it's more like a spirituality thing that creates a method for looking into ourselves by observing someone who is, in a way, just like us.

We may often have a mental compulsion, an attraction to personalities that are so different from ours that they seem like a puzzle—something to be investigated further and discovered. This is sometimes why we end up forming bonds with people like this so we can hopefully be let in on the big secret.

In reality, there is scarcely a secret to be learned. These mysterious personalities we come into contact with daily are usually merely a reflection of our own mysterious nature.

After all, we learn to connect in a variety of ways. Whether it be through speech, written form, or a more modern method of emails and text messaging, which allows us to connect on a more massive scale as compared to those methods of communication available to past generations.

But, why are we so drawn to these types? What in our brain pushes us almost magnetically to these types of people who seem so mysterious, so standoffish, and might actually prove to be a danger?

In the world of the human mind, most of the territory is uncharted. Most metaphysical questions we have about the world around us— and the world ahead of us—are yet unanswered. We are constantly yearning for answers to these questions, no matter how desperately we have to search for them. After all, humans will do almost anything for knowledge.

Think about the last time you read a particularly intriguing novel, for which you were incredibly curious to know the ending. Something in you said to just stick it out and wait until you progressed naturally to the end of the story. That way, you could have all the clues, all the enriching information that would surely enhance the revelation of the solution to all the characters' problems.

And yet, the call of knowing the answer you ask was so alluring. It would be so unbelievably easy to just flip to the end of the book. You wouldn't have to go through all the trouble of looking through all the gristle of the story when all you really want is the satisfaction of knowing how it all ends.

So, you flip. You flip and flip and skim through the last few pages, and you find the end. The resolution is so satisfying, but what's even more satisfying than the ending is the fact that now you know how it ends. You can say you have that knowledge. Even though you don't actually know what happened to reach that ending, you're satisfied with the fact of the matter; you now have the answer to what you had been asking at the beginning of the story. That alone is often enough to stave off the lingering guilt of skipping the bulk of the novel.

If you choose to rush the process of the story, you follow a trend of curiosity and restlessness. We as a species, especially over the past few decades, have become increasingly impatient. You may want to blame this change on the development of a system where we only need to wait about five seconds for any information we want to be delivered to us on a screen. We are beings who want the answers. We don't necessarily want the context that may or may not enrich that knowledge. The pride of comprehension often outweighs any moral satisfaction we might get from following the "rules."

How can we apply this knowledge to our interactions with people, especially enigmatic individuals whose actions too often elude us?

This book will help educate you further on ways to go about interacting with such people, from understanding their motives to being able to read them before they're able to even read themselves.

Oftentimes, behind the mask of a mysterious stranger is someone who is simply different than us who we struggle to empathize with based only on our current knowledge. It is often not someone on another level or on another planet, or some mysterious person who's been trained in the art of deception. These fairytales we tell ourselves are usually to make up for the actual more mundane explanations that we find when we pull back the mask on this person.

In this book, you will be exposed to ways of pulling back these kinds of masks and taking an interrogative look at the individual that hides beneath them. We often find ourselves fascinated with the art of reading people, likely driven by our desire, our addiction to knowledge. And what can be more interesting and enrapturing to the human mind aside from another human mind? There are so many different kinds of people, and each individual within those categories acts for their own unique reasons with their own motivations. This book is about being able to accurately estimate what context might be behind the way a person acts and how to use the skills you find in that process to aid in all other areas of your life, including personal and business relationships and internal concepts you may have on a more philosophical level. The art of psychoanalysis can cover all of these bases and more, as you'll soon find out as you read further.

Chapter Two: The Art of a Category

As humans, we come into contact with many different kinds of people every day. Unless, of course, you have obtained this book while also living completely off-grid or are otherwise totally separated from society, you will likely come into contact with more individuals than you realize every day, each one different. Humans are said to be like snowflakes; despite our massive similarities, we are all incredibly different from one another, retaining many small features that come together to craft an individual.

In this book, a range of topics will be covered, all pertaining to different methods of analyzing people. Before you can better understand the people around you, you have to first understand yourself. To be able to analyze yourself accurately shows that you have a base knowledge on how people work internally and how those internal functions come together to create the outward mannerisms of a person.

Before beginning, let's preface the subject matter with this; analyzing people is not a superpower. It's an ability that any person, and every person, can easily learn, a skill to be honed over time and with practice. As with any skill, there are those people who have a natural aptitude for analyzing people around them. Individuals with natural talents are not necessarily always going to be better at analysis once skills are learned. On the contrary, often those with innate skill don't feel the need to hone their talent, and will, therefore, be surpassed by their peers who move forward through practiced skill. So, don't be discouraged by someone who seems to naturally understand other people.

Psychoanalysis is not a power to be used for malicious purposes. Many people do not have pure intentions while learning how to "read" people. In fact, some people plan to use their skills to manipulate others to their will or will simply use it for selfish or potentially dangerous purposes.

Humans tend to be oddly open to others at times, whether they mean to be or not. It's important to keep in mind that, no matter how open a person may be, the person you may be looking to analyze will be cognizant. Most people have a general understanding of their own conduct themselves and what that might say about them. If you are obviously looking to analyze someone in order to manipulate them for your purposes, they will likely soon become aware of your intentions. Of course, ideally, your moral compass would be enough to drive you away from the idea of taking such blatant advantage of an innocent person.

Some of the content that will be covered in this book includes:

- The secrets behind personality types
- Body language
- Emotional intelligence
- Persuasion
- The basics of behavioral psychology
- Manipulation (i.e. persuading someone with malevolent intentions)
- The art of psychoanalysis and speed-reading people and behavior

If one or more of these things grabs your attention, you're in luck. If these things pique your interest, you are likely someone who is curious or on a constant search for truth and honesty from people. You may like the idea of having a heart-to-heart conversation with someone, whether they be a loved one or a total stranger. You may like to quickly get down to the nitty-gritty of a person and their beliefs. If these things apply to you, congratulations! You've just been analyzed. Fast analysis like this, also referred to by some as rapid cognition, is not always as accurate as long, more drawn-out naturalistic observation, but it tends to be fairly accurate for the few seconds it takes to perform the analysis. Just by showing that you're interested enough in the art of analyzing people and further understanding psychology to read this far into this book, you've grouped yourself in with other people that exhibit interests similar to you.

You may naturally assume that individuals with interests similar to yours also share a similar set of personality traits. You may do this without meaning to, just like everyone else groups themselves in with other people. Because humans are pack animals, creatures that feel the most at peace, the most at home when they're with people they identify with, we often accidentally make ourselves easy to categorize.

We are all individual people with special parts of ourselves that set us apart from every single other person on the planet. Our similarities also have the undeniable power to bring us together. Of these similarities, perhaps one of the most adhesive bonds between all people is our willingness and ability to categorize ourselves, whether this takes place in our physicality (our blood type, eye color, etc.), or within more psychologically focused categories. These categories would include things like personality types, interests, education, class, race, gender, sexuality, and many other things we use to put the world and its inhabitants neatly into "perfect little boxes" in our minds.

Sometimes, these neat boxes can do more harm than good. Think about how many news articles and movies you've seen about members of a demographic attempting to break free of the expectations on them because of existing categories. Consider someone of a different demographic trying to break into the world of a marginalized group of people and trying to pull others into that world, a world where people are given more of a chance. When thinking of this kind of media, you might think of movies or news stories that focus on race or on people below the poverty line, but this kind of narrative can be constructed from any demographic. 'Break the mold' stories are often written because the related issues and divisions draw the most attention.

To better understand the categories we so swiftly seem to place ourselves and our peers in, let's look to a popular example: a fascination with personality tests.

Take, for a more specific example, the Myers-Briggs Type Indicator (MBTI), more often referred to as the 16 personalities test. This test measures your personality and the way you present yourself to the world with five facets:

> 1. Your extraversion or introversion: This aspect reflects how energetically you interact with others, and whether you recharge mentally better alone or in a group.
> 2. Your skills of observation and intuition: This aspect compares whether you like to make decisions by watching others closely, or if you are more likely to improvise and go with the flow.
> 3. Thinking vs. feeling: This is one of the more popularly analyzed traits of any person. When making an important decision, do you rely more on your emotional compass or on your reasoning skills? Do you think it's important to respect the views of your peers, even if the factual information you may have doesn't align with their ideas? These are some of the questions that go into determining where you fall on the scale.

4. Judging or prospecting: The forth aspect is reflected with questions that measure to what degree you take the initiative in a social setting, as well as whether or not you would be fit for a leadership or CEO role in your work life.

5. Finally, at the end of your personality type, you will receive a dash, followed by "A" or "T." This letter indicates whether you have a more assertive or turbulent personality. In other words, whether you're the kind of person who leads the pack or if you prefer to linger in the background watching and learning before you take a decisive first step.

All of these things combined make up your MBTI personality type, and this is only one method you can easily find online of evaluating yourself and your motivations in life.

For example, one person's personality type according to the Myer-Briggs scale might be ENFP-T, also known as the "campaigner" personality. This the personality type dislikes being categorized yet loves to categorize others. The quiz also will tell someone of this personality type that they may be the kind of person who looks at life through a very analytical lens, yet one that is tinted with passion and emotion. A person of this category may view life as a massive and complicated puzzle and have made it their life's mission to solve that puzzle. The quiz usually takes about ten minutes.

This may all seem very dramatic for a 10-minute test to tell you, but personality tests work this way at their core. They ask similar questions to help gauge your personality through a range of information. Although not every test will use the Myer-Briggs scale of defining one's personality, most personality tests, at least most of the reputable ones, will use roughly the same template of questions. This is because there are only so many ways to gauge someone's personality based on their tendencies, or at least their tendencies that they're consciously aware of and that can be recorded online via a personality test that takes anywhere from 60 seconds to 15 minutes.

So, if almost every personality test you take is pretty much the same and likely going to give you an identical result, why do you find yourself compelled to take them?

The overwhelming majority of personality tests and quizzes you can take online may just reiterate to you glaring matters you already knew about yourself. If this is the case, why do so many people find it so fun to take them?

We want to be validated. Each person, no matter their walk of life, likely is at least a somewhat interested in self-validation. This isn't really a single person or source's doing. The environment we are being raised in, from our parents and peers to our favorite shows or the news our parents watch, has slowly turned us into a society full of young people who feel a need to be validated. For some, validation from a peer can be more exciting that a promotion or a raise.

Validation and verification are a little too important to everyone in the modern era. We look to quite literally any personality test to determine things we already probably could've told someone about ourselves. How extraverted or introverted we are, whether we're more suited for hot or cold climates based on our personalities, what animal we are most like based on the traits gained in a quiz from a website that took less than five minutes to complete.

We've nearly lost the ability to deeply reflect on ourselves. Instead, even our own philosophy is something we are consistently checking with others to make sure we're on the ball. So, recognizing this problem, how do we stop it? How do we stop something that's been ingrained in our heads pretty much since birth?

Personality tests are helpful, and they do have their place in helping understand our own tendencies. Sometimes when we take them though, we may not understand the questions, leaving us with less than accurate results. We may also find that none of the answers fit us or our preferences, again leaving us with only partially accurate results. Instead, why not live your life based on you, the main character of your own life?

We often have trouble looking inward because we fear being wrong and having our internal struggle exposed. We've also lost the confidence to tell ourselves that the path we're on is correct, even without anyone else to verify that statement. It's so incredibly difficult to try and assure yourself, especially when you've had someone by your side holding your metaphorical hand just about every single step of the way prior to that.

In short, the only real way you can cut the strings trapping your heart and mind is to start forcing yourself to look inward! This book will help you learn how to do this. After all, to first understand someone else's motives, you have to first understand your own. This book will teach you how to analyze and quickly read people, but it will not tell you exactly what is right and wrong.

It's up to you to determine how the information fits your life; it's your responsibility to answer some of your own questions that this book will bring to light for you. Using the knowledge you obtain while reading coupled with the knowledge you already have about yourself and the people around you can help you better interact with others.

Chances are, you probably didn't even know some of that inner knowledge existed. When we have something in front of us to rely on, like a personality quiz, instead of being left strictly to our own internal selves, those devices start to work less and work slower. Like any other machine, our brain won't work at its top efficiency, if we aren't utilizing its power often enough. The more you rely on outside opinions for your validation instead of relying on yourself and thinking about your own actions in an objective way, the lazier your brain will become and the more difficult it will be when you're left with no choice to think about yourself.

So, the next time you see an appealing link to a personality test, no matter how reputable or valuable the information may seem in that moment, take a moment and think about the question that you want to be answered. Chances are, you can answer the question about yourself more accurately than any test can.

The other great thing about gaining philosophical information about yourself is theorizing. In short, you are your own science experiment in a way. Use yourself as your experiments, your hypotheses, your data, in any way you see fit. If you want a question answered that you think you can answer for yourself, look inward and see if you can answer it!

Take for example Emmett. Emmett is a very compassionate and empathetic person, and he's usually trying to make connections with his peers. By doing this, Emmett makes beneficial and long-lasting connections quickly, which makes him happy, and the cycle of connection continues.

However, Emmett wonders why he gets such a kick out of making these connections. Usually, they don't really benefit him personally in a way proportionate to how enthusiastically he makes those very same connections. He knows he isn't doing it out of selfishness because he isn't just making connections with people in positions of power or people who will benefit his standing in life or work. So, why is he doing it?

To answer this question, let's take a closer look at how Emmett makes the outstanding connections that he does. He does this by keeping in touch with almost everyone he meets and attending social outings whenever possible. When he is at these social outings, he often becomes very attached to people very quickly, and this affection that people receive from him is welcome. It is often welcome enough that the person receiving gives Emmett plenty of affection in return. When Emmett receives this surplus of affection in return, he becomes happier and therefore more affectionate, leading that circle to continue itself and the connection made to strengthen.

Now, what does Emmett's methods of connection building reflect about him as a person? You may have taken note of the fact that Emmett is a very affectionate person. This compliments that he is extraverted compared to some of his peers and is also much better at making connections simply because he goes out and interacts with others. However, his reasoning goes deeper than that, to a fairly selfish place that is commonplace in many extraverted people.

You likely also took note that Emmett became much happier when he received attention and affection in return for his own. Although this is a very normal response to the affection that you would expect of essentially anyone, what it actually says about him is very telling.

You see, the reason Emmett becomes so excited and happy when he receives positive attention and affection from others is because that's exactly why he gave it in the first place.

Although Emmett genuinely enjoys seeing people be happy and enjoy themselves, a small part of why he is so interactive and engaging is because he craves attention. He gives out large amounts of affection to people because he wants them to like him, which will make him feel more secure in his accomplishments and in himself as a whole.

Using Emmett as an example is simply shedding light on the fact that humans are often selfish creatures. We aren't really evil, but we are selfish. Some may wish to think of being selfish as a neutral, albeit unattractive trait. We're often far too absorbed in our own issues to even begin to think of interacting in the life of someone else. But you see, it's this selfish and stagnant way of thinking that traps a person and it traps many people for extended periods of time. It'd hard not to get trapped in that cycle, but it's not impossible to break out of it.

As you contemplate yourself, don't be afraid to break out of your shell. You don't need anyone else's help to understand who you are as a person. This book will give you the basics for getting started. After that, it's up to you. Categories exist in the human mind, but they're not meant to contain everyone. You are a person of your own unique design, with the power to do whatever you want with your abilities, should you choose to improve them by reading and learning further.

Chapter Three: Looking Inward

The art of psychoanalysis has to begin inwardly. This might seem a little counterproductive to people who just want to begin understanding the people around them in much better focus. However, it simply isn't that streamlined.

Think of how many people who have preached that "to love someone else, you have to first love yourself." Not only is this sentiment true, but the same concept also holds true for just about everything. Whatever you want to apply to others, you have to first be able to steadily apply to yourself, if only to better understand what you're applying in the first place.

For example, let's say you want to know what that enigmatic coworker or mysterious mutual friend is thinking. Their thoughts and actions seem totally unreadable, and you're dying to know just what makes them tick.

To be able to understand this person, you have to first be able to analyze yourself. Looking inward, think of some things you seem to do on autopilot. What choices do you make with your subconscious without really taking the time to thoroughly weigh your options? Think of ways that people have seemed confused by your actions.

There is not anyone who is truly unreadable. It's more than likely that to someone else, you are actually the mysterious and enigmatic peer or colleague.

Knowing this and collecting information on your own actions and tendencies—whether they be patterns you are consciously aware of, or habits that the people around you pick up on before you do— analyze them. Ask those around you who are in a position where they observe you often, a work friend or your spouse, where they perceive those actions might originate. The real secret to developing your ability to read people is knowing how to stockpile the basics on analysis and put them to practical work in the real world. No one will be as easy for you to psychoanalyze as you are.

Now that you've collected information, it's time to put it to use in the real world. Make connections. The hidden source of some of your tendencies may actually be the source of someone else's tendencies as well. Although every person's exact situation is obviously different, there are often similarities between those who have a positive relationship with each other; similarities may be observed on a deeper level, as well as on the surface of a relationship.

Say, for example, that you and a friend have similarly aggressive personalities. You don't really feel malicious or that you are acting aggressively, but people tell you that you drive people away because of your behavior. Even though you don't perceive it as necessarily aggressive or intend for it to be that way, it simply comes off as combative and overly defensive. Why might this be? You see that people say the same thing about your friend, and you can see why. So, if these traits are glaring in both you and your friend, but you're both very sure that you aren't secretly malicious or mean-spirited people who have a vendetta against those around you, what's actually going on?

Luckily for you and your friend, those traits don't indicate psychopathy or that you're secretly evil. In fact, oftentimes those traits indicate the opposite; that you're scared and emotionally malnourished.

People that come off unintentionally as combative of defensive tend to really just be looking for safety. They feel threatened by the situation around them and have their fight-or-flight response almost constantly activated. This is why we perceive them as so on their guard all the time. They may be afraid of being involved in a potentially scary or dangerous situation, even if the context of their actual situation doesn't fit that narrative of events at all.

Although there are several different potential causes of this kind of behavior, the most common one falls under the umbrella of past trauma—a cause that will pop up very often if you read a lot of different kinds of people. Someone who is overly defensive and combative is often simply scared, whether they're afraid of confrontation or afraid of being emotionally vulnerable. The specifics will vary based on each person and your experiences with them, but this only serves as a general outline for this specific kind of behavior. Those who display this kind of hidden fear have usually been hurt in the past, likely scarred emotionally by someone they trusted with an emotional wound from which they never really healed. The person's father or mother may not have been in the picture or was neglectful or cold or possibly abusive. The child develops an unconscious yearning for that kind of parental bonding that they never received at home. They were deprived of that form of love and affection and will seek it out in their adult life through any means necessary.

Applying this way of thinking to the example regarding aggression, it's easy to deduce that you and your friend share your combative tendencies because you may not have been taught how to empathize. This kind of behavior will actually more often stem from a non-present mother figure, not a father one. Although this doesn't apply to every home, mothers tend to be the parent more often at home with the child, emotionally bonding with them, giving them warm advice, etc. When this kind of nurturing treatment is not present in a child's life, they grow up not knowing how to empathize and usually feel insecure in the world and with themselves.

So, you've figured out the answer! Humans tend to be like an emotional puzzle, full of contextual evidence and twists and turns that will eventually lead you to a rather complicated answer. Don't let seemingly complex people discourage you from investigating. The point of analysis is, ideally, to help the people around you by helping them understand why they feel the way they do and how to combat the negative feelings they have. Understand that you, as a friend or acquaintance, are not meant to replace clinical help, but anyone with a warm enough heart to make the choice to try and help someone is also always a massive aid to those emotionally in need.

This was, of course, just an example. It can't be applied to everyone, even in that more specific scenario of a particularly combative individual. Sometimes combative and defensive people grow up in fine, loving homes, and develop their combative tendencies from another event entirely. This is completely possible and shouldn't be thrown out simply because you think you know a person's reasoning. Psychological analysis is not, an exact science. It's a good way to estimate why someone feels the way they do and begin to understand more about yourself and about the people around you.

Analysis becomes more precise when used on yourself. Using this information on yourself is a good way to gain insight into yourself and why you act a certain way or express yourself through a certain medium. Again, while it certainly isn't an exact science, it's a way to look inward in a way you likely haven't in the past. It's a way that allows you to look inside yourself in a more spiritual way and help you be at peace with yourself, whether through understanding yourself or seeking outside aid for your emotional struggle.

To reiterate, analyzing and understanding your problems or someone else's problems will not fix them for you or for that person. The only thing that can really push an individual forward in the sense of helping them heal is action. Understanding that someone acts combative because they feel unloved is a massive first step but knowing this won't change their actions. What will change their actions is making them feel loved and supported, like they aren't alone.

If you or someone you know experiences suicidal thoughts or thoughts that warrant genuine fear for his or her safety or the safety of others, taking action by yourself isn't enough. Contact medical help or the police if you find yourself in a situation where someone's life or safety is at risk. Again, taking action by yourself just isn't enough to protect yourself or others, no matter how much you might like to think that you can save someone on your own. Don't play the hero. Get yourself or that person help if you feel it is warranted.

Looking inward isn't always such a serious matter, however. As I said before, it can also take the place of one of your favorite personality tests. Learning about yourself isn't a grim or scary experience, it's an enriching one that can tell you things about yourself that you may not have understood or connected with in the past.

For instance, let's set you back in the shoes of someone who displays distancing behavior. You may feel absolutely no motivation, obsessive, or combative and like you're being overly defensive. You know from reading this book, and simply from past experiences, that distancing behavior isn't produced from nothing. If you feel as though it may be causing yourself or others issue, or you simply want to know where this divergent tendency might come from, ask yourself the following questions:

- Have I always acted like this? If not, when did it start?
- Are there certain situations in which this tendency or habit flares up? Does it get worse during stress? Or when I'm around large crowds or certain types of people? Is there a certain person or specific people that trigger it?
- Ask yourself questions about your current situation. Does this pertain to your finances, your personal life, your job,

your current emotional state, or your relationship. Do any of these things influence the tendencies or habits you may have noticed?

Ask yourself these questions, as applicable, and other questions that you may come up with that are tailored more specifically to your situation. Asking yourself questions is one of the ways to stockpile information about yourself in the most efficient way possible. After stockpiling this info, it can be applied to most other people around you. After all, no matter the root of your issues, there are likely many people around you who are suffering in a way very similar to you!

In summary, you have to be able to analyze yourself before you can truly analyze anyone else. You are the person whose patterns and habits are most easily predicted by you, so use that to your advantage! Making yourself a lab rat for your own psychological experiments is a good way to better understand your colleagues who may act similarly to you. Being able to understand the way you act and the root of those behaviors is the first and debatably the most important step toward being able to read and better understand others on a deeply psychological and emotional level.

Never experiment on yourself in a way that may be harmful to yourself or others. The point of analyzing people is not to break them down or take them apart for the sake of understanding them. One of the most avid users of psychoanalysis and speed-reading people are therapists and social workers, people whose job depends on their ability to help and comfort people who are feeling complex or scary emotions. Understand that the emotions you're feeling are in no way scary, no matter how intimidating of massive they may feel. Your feelings are a vital part of your human identity, as well as your identity as an individual. Knowing this should not be intimidating; if anything, it should be empowering to know that you've taken control of your emotions and therefore, of your life!

However, some who have an innate understanding of how to analyze people look at individuals through a scope, eyeing people as machines more so than as people with feelings. Some people who never had an opportunity to learn what they were seeing through that visual scope simply adopted a cynical way of thinking; the rate of individuals who are good at reading others tends to match the rate of cynics and pessimists today. Keeping this in mind, try to move forward while you hone your abilities. Remember that the people around you are not your science experiments; they are not for you to play with or to manipulate to your will for malicious purposes. Treat others with the same respect that you desire from them.

Some might wonder where this persona similar to an individual with a god complex might actually originate. This, in and of itself, is a test of someone's ability to analyze the ones around them. Say you suffer from something similar to this god complex. Maybe you feel that since you can analyze other people, you have some kind of cruel advantage over them, some overwhelming power that you alone can exert over people at will. Whether this is actually true or not is irrelevant. You may hold an innate ability to understand other people's emotions but struggle to comprehend your own.

This personality type might sound familiar to you, it might not. It might even be an accurate reflection of your personality, or at least of the persona you put up toward others, When people act this way they may have some kind of façade they hope to keep, whether that façade is of superior or intelligence or simply of power.

A general rule of thumb when analyzing or reading people is that as adults we may yearn for something we severely lacked during childhood. This is why so many people who are overly clingy or affectionate end up emotionally malnourished. They may easily drive people away without meaning to or even knowing they have done so. This may become a cycle of falling deeper and deeper into despair, a cycle that is very, very difficult to crawl out of when you are someone who is unaware of the problem, even at the most basic level.

So, if you or someone you know shows problematic signs or patterns in behavior, what can be done to prevent or stop it? Overcoming an inner personality complex can be especially difficult. When someone suffers from a narcissistic personality or a is often self-focused, they may have a very hard time believing that they have a problem. Similar to the stereotypical drug addict, smoker, or local news story the victim may feel as though there is no possible situation in which they are in the wrong, and grabs hold of that train of thought, that believe, perhaps until they can no longer recover.

This trait is common in people who suffer from some a personality disorder, such as antisocial personality disorder—a disorder in which the sufferer feels little to no remorse or grief for their actions, and finds it impossible to empathize, let alone sympathize with others. Narcissistic personality disorder, or NPD, is characterized simply by the victim being obsessed with maintaining their societal image through power, appearances, money, materialism, and retaining an extreme and uncommonly sensitive sense of ego and belonging in the world. These disorders are relatively uncommon in the general populous, but the traits are more common than many would care to admit.

If the symptoms are so wide-spread, how is it that people with narcissistic tendencies and similar afflictions aren't getting the help they clearly need? Consent laws have an effect on who gets help. Individuals who feel they do not need to seek help cannot be forcefully helped unless as a byproduct of committing a crime. If the person is a minor, it is possible for them to be directed by a family member or guardian.

If you wish to help someone without fighting to get them the care they need, keep in mind that individuals may feel the need to assert dominance at all times, even to themselves, to stay in the control. They may seem self-assured, but it usually isn't particularly difficult to knock someone like this down to earth. "Knocking them down" isn't exactly the go-to method when dealing with someone who is self-focused.   When they are proven wrong in a way that is irrefutable, they may shut down, argue nonsensically, become volatile, or dangerous. Keep this readily in mind when dealing with someone of this nature.

In general, people that feel the need to constantly assert authority—authority they may or may not actually possess—need to be slowly and calmly brought down from the euphoria of their delusional behavior. Asserting false power or authority can be the equivalent of a hyper-fueled sugar rush, so quickly revoking that dopamine rush from the individual might result in a withdrawal of emotions. They may be simply accustomed to the sensation of feeling as though they are dominating a person or a group of people. They will often need to be gradually weaned off that high, just like someone with a physical addiction.

Now that you're more readily equipped with the skills needed to psychologically assess yourself, as well as the basics of assessing others, let's dive deeper into the mainframe of the human psyche, to offer a better and more cohesive insight into analyzing people.

Chapter Four: Human Body's Language

Perhaps the most acutely fascinating topic when dealing with psychoanalysis is body language and other physical cues that can be picked up on when reading someone. Even if you lack the necessary background knowledge to read a person, don't know them well enough to get an accurate portrayal of their behaviors, or are not great at picking up on subtler cues, reading someone's body language is perhaps the easiest way to quickly and stealthily begin to understand other people.

Neurotypical individuals—that is to say, those who don't fall under the autism spectrum—have an innate, seemingly built in basic understanding of how people position themselves and what their positioning can mean in the context of society and conversation with others. We unknowingly build this reservoir of information up from the moment we begin to comprehend images, from watching our parents to watching strangers everywhere we go, even as infants and toddlers. This trend leads us to our adult phases of life, where we have a library of knowledge about people's physical cues and body language; a library that many of us didn't even know we had.

Of course, to begin discussing body language, we have to first talk about the entire body as a whole first. When someone is engaging in conversation, and has their entire body facing toward another person, makes direct and frequent eye contact, and is generally responsive, it's likely that the individual trusts the person with whom they are conversing. It may also be that they are someone who feels safe in that environment and who is secure with themselves. Someone who is very closed off physically and lacks expressiveness and emotion in their voice and pose, may feel insecure or uncomfortable with either the other person or the location. Of course, these are two extremes on the elongated an in-depth spectrum of body language, posturing, and tone.

A tell-tale sign of the way a person is feeling is the positioning of their arms. Noticing this without staring at the person or otherwise seeming suspicious can be helpful. The way someone's arms are positioned can tell you a lot about the way a person perceives their current situation. One physical way of defending ourselves from potential danger is by using our arms. When you fall forward, how do you instinctively try to catch yourself? The answer is likely with your arms. Keeping this in mind, there are many ways a person's arm positioning can indicate their mood, general personality, and other things about them:

> • Arms at side: This is obviously a very neutral pose. What this pose indicates depends heavily on the context of what the rest of the person's physicality is communicating. Another giveaway which adds context to this pose is what other poses they are shifting through the person's stance. For example, if a person has his arms at his sides, and every now and then shifts them to his pockets or similar, it's likely a sign that this person is acting casual and overall is feeling relaxed. However, if they are shifting quickly between this seemingly neutral pose and moving their hands between their lap and pockets, they may feel impatient. They may also simply be in a place or position where they're expected to act formally,

especially if they wouldn't normally act this way. These rules aren't concrete, but this is a trend that follows most people, so it's treated as a general rule of thumb.

• Arms crossed: This is usually a telltale sign that a person feels defensive, or as if they're being attacked. This position is usually taken by someone who is insecure with themselves or their situation and wants to feel in control and unbothered by physically asserting this through their body language. This position may also be a simple neutral or relaxed state—some people just position their arms this way out of habit or because they don't know what else they should be doing with their arms. Don't read too deeply into what may look like a different story than reality. Again, rely on other context clues and signals from body language to piece the case together.

• Hand scratching at neck or face: Someone who repeatedly scratching the neck or face may be anxious, as though they are helpless, or otherwise not at all in control of the situation. A similar gesture to note is rubbing the thumb over the side of the forefinger while making something of a fist. This gesture is sometimes used by people when they feel as though they need to comfort themselves. Again, these things might simply be nervous tendencies and are not directly related to an event immediately at hand. No situation is the same, observe the situation for proper context.

Another part of the body that is a much subtler but still a defining giveaway for a person's behavior is the positioning of their feet. For instance, say you were at a party and saw three people in a triangle conversing about something. The first person has one foot pointed in the general direction of both of the other participants in the conversation. The second person also has both their feet pointed toward both other people, indicating that they are paying full attention to both other people. The third person, however, has both feet pointed toward one person, instead of one of their feet at either person. This indicates that this person is not actually paying full attention to both people but is only paying real attention to one of the other participants.

As another example, if you see someone standing at a desk— whether it be to check in at a hotel or to order coffee—the direction their foot is pointing indicates which way they are likely going to take their next step. Although someone's footing may seem overly subtle and inconsequential, these tiny details actually come together to create a full image of a person's body language.

Something else to be noted regarding body gestures is the way a person reacts physically. It's not only the smaller parts alone that matter, but the bigger picture of the way an individual speaks, moves, and generally conducts themselves. For instance, someone nodding or otherwise bobbing their head while listening to a conversation is usually showing attentiveness. However, the actual context of this behavior can depend from person to person, especially in how they feel about the person with whom they are conversating. An individual who is showing vigorous signs of agreement to someone in a position of authority or someone they respect, revere, or even fear, may wish to garner that person's favor. They may be falsifying a sense of camaraderie to get themselves onto the other person's good side, even if they are not aware of their actions.

Someone who is slouched or partially turned away from a person they are talking to may do so out of anxiety or fear toward that person. Someone who simply slouches on their own, without the external stimulus of someone else to cause them to act this way, may be someone who seems suspicious but is in reality an anxious and massively insecure person.

This brings us to some of the umbrellas of human behavior and how different people might present themselves through their behavior. For example, there are many different kinds of people who will present different ways when they feel unsecure with themselves. The way they present themselves will heavily depend on their background, the actual source of their insecurity, the kind of environment in which they were raised, and sometimes may rely at least partially on genetics. Someone who was raised in an environment where showing weakness was heavily discouraged, the person will likely grow into a teenager and then an adult who does not display emotion. If a child was made to feel lesser or weaker for acting emotionally vulnerable or empathetic, they may also be unable to respond well in emotional situations. Because they have no real healthy image of empathy and strength, they will almost always treat others the way they were treated in childhood. These are those individuals who will put you down for reaching out to others and actively try and make those around them feel embarrassed for having genuine interests or feelings. They may greatly benefit from therapy interactions. They need to be exposed to the concepts of letting their metaphorical walls down and being emotionally open to people they trust. However, having trust may be a foreign concept on its own to people who have been emotionally abused or neglected in the past, whether that abuse took place during childhood or not.

Other people who are insecure with themselves may present this in a more obvious way. They may have never had the support system of friends or family to teach them how to cope with the world and the people around them. They may view themselves as overly emotional, or too vulnerable compared to their peers. They will be emotionally and physically closed off, from themselves and from the world as well. They will also be in a kind of emotionally dead state, unable to handle their emotions because they were never taught how to communicate them to others and deal with them in a safe and healthy way. These are not the traits of an abused child, but a neglected child; a child who was never coddled, never comforted, and likely never supported. These individuals also would ideally be exposed to some kind of therapy or outside help, but for some that is unattainable for at least some time. These individuals need to be shown love and compassion. Usually, it is easier to work with someone who is emotionally closed off and shy than it is to work with someone who is emotionally closed off but does not recognize that they have a problem. This reaches back into the subject of individuals with something of a self-focused perspective who don't know quite how to communicate with others and who may have no intention of trying to learn.

Insecurity is often the root of most divergently minded behavior; although, many behaviors could be labeled either divergent or typical, depending on your outlook. Insecurity is a profound source of strange and uncomfortable behavior in society today. Why is that?

Insecurity has been ingrained in our brains. From our parents nagging us for good grades to all the bad news you could ever imagine, security in our abilities, in our rank, in our place in the world, has been more severely malnourished than ever. It's become an epidemic in every demographic, although the problem is admittedly much more widespread in younger groups of people. What can we do to combat this insecurity? Why does it seem to pop up now more than in the past? Has so much really changed in the way we perform our daily rituals?

The answer is not as simple as some might prefer; it's been lurking behind the door of every generation who has been taught it is nearly a sin to be anything but headstrong and viciously secure in themselves. Now that we've moved past all of the parents and grandparents who have subconsciously learned to drown their feelings and fears, we're at a young, bright generation who never had those same headstrong teachings. The ones that have had those teachings, rejected it. We're currently living in a time full of passion and turmoil, both of which are fighting vigorously to be unrestricted.

To return to the subject of body language and other subtle physical insights to the human psyche, let's take a bit of an analytical look at voice toning. The tone of a person's voice can portray perhaps too much about a person's life. With the right kind of equipment and a professional, you can often even tell a person's stature and some physical attributes, simply from a their voice.

Listening to someone's conversation may seem like a morally questionable thing to do, but simply listening to someone you're conversing with may bring greater understanding regarding how you perceive them and how much you know about that person.

Say you knew someone who seemed outgoing, vivacious, lively, perhaps even overly confident to the point of arrogance. And yet, they stumble over their words almost constantly. This does not refer to a stutter or some other speech impediment; speech impediments fall under the title of things that are usually out of the control of the individual.

No, this person simply stumbles over all of their words, every time, every single sentence. It's hard to try and understand why because this person just seems to ooze confidence and gusto. The may retain the demeanor of someone who knows their stuff and even more so knows how to prove it. And, yet they stumble.

So, what's going on here? Going back to human insecurity and the vast epidemic it's become today all around the world. Many people who put up a façade are not extreme examples, but normal people in our everyday lives that lack a support system, the motivation, or simply the direction and guidance to build up their confidence naturally. Because of this, many people often adopt a "fake it 'til you make it" mentality, and may merely fake their confidence instead of actually possessing it. This is much faster than actually figuring out how to discard your insecurities and has relatively the same effect as the real you does in society. Although this kind of coping and defense mechanism isn't without some merit, a large number of people utilize it at some point in their lives as they learn to support themselves emotionally. However, being able to do this requires not only using the "fake it 'til you make it" mindset, but also requires you to put in a lot of your own time, energy, and dedication for it to even begin to work in your favor.

Many people don't exactly understand this—or at least, fail to understand it well enough to apply it to their lives consistently—and end up in a kind of never-ending loop for a large portion of their lives. You may be faking an entire charade and hiding behind it in the hopes that you'll be perceived as a competent, outgoing, and competent person.

Again, like many kinds of behavior, hiding behind a façade can almost always be traced back to a crippling fear of loneliness, abandonment, or more centrally, a fear appearing weak. These fears are commonplace, especially in young people in this modern era of being afraid to be emotionally weak in front people we revere or admire.

At any rate, this person stumbles over their words, indicating that maybe that confidence they ooze isn't so genuine after all. It's very possible that it's all an act they're trying to keep up. Body language is a bit easier to force and check yourself on than your voice. As natural as the way we carry ourselves is, it's easy to pay attention to body placement when you're around others. Your voice, however, is much more natural and freely moving through you, so it can be more difficult to keep your voice in check without making it seem forced. Stumbling over words can communicate consistent uncertainty in decisions or opinions, which is a dead giveaway that the person speaking is fairly unconfident in themselves, no matter what their posturing or "personality" as publicly portrayed.

Which leads us to another quick but still relevant bit of information about a few sociological notes we will review about current and past generations. The personality of a human being is a lot more fluid than you might think.

In ancient Japanese folklore, it was said we had three personalities, or "faces." The first face was our public one, the way we presented ourselves to the world and to our acquaintances. The second face was a bit more "real" to life, the personality we present to our loved ones, our friends and family who are particularly close to us. This was also considered the mask that we presented to our spouses. The third mask was the most intimate: the mask of self. This was the personality that was never, could never, be seen by anyone else in the world except for its wearer. This is what was said to remain when the other two masks fell away, so to speak. What we were left with was the true self.

Although a tad bit old-fashioned, it may be that the shogun and the samurai were on to something. You'll likely hear in your lifetime, that someone feels so caught up in the "masks" that they show to the world and to their loved ones, that when those masks are removed, it feels as if there's simply nothing left. They may feel as if they have no distinguishable personality outside what they show others, what they show to the world.

This says something about how we've changed throughout the years. If you're currently reading this book and are below the age of 35, you may or may not identify with this feeling of being so out of place with yourself that when you're on your own with no one else to entertain you, you feel that there's simply nothing left to observe. Like there is no true "you." What are you without the distractions of your everyday routine, the rut that so many people feel so trapped irreversibly by?

Let's cut to the chase; many people feel out of touch inwardly because they fail to practice self-searching on their own time. This goes back to our much earlier topic of why personality tests are not as helpful as some people want them to be. They don't prepare us for situations in life where we will inevitably have to look inward at ourselves objectively and understand ourselves in a way that helps us connect both to ourselves and to those around us. Without that practice, the unnecessary guidance of other sources and third parties acts as a crutch for us. It lets us escape the uncomfortable sensation of searching ourselves and accepting our flaws as people. With this knowledge in hand, let's move forward while we work to understand further the depths of psychoanalysis and how to better your skills.

Chapter Five: What Humans Hold Inside

Behavioral psychologists and sociologists often discuss the origin of the nature of humans. Some feel that humans are not inherently good, or inherently evil. Some people feel that we are born with certain features one way or another, simply because we are descendants of those who came before us. The debate about how humans learn to make choices develops is as vast as the oceans.

Sometimes people like to suggest that humans are inherently evil, bound to do evil and cruel things simply because they feel the momentary and fleeting whim to perform that action. No one does something "bad," simply because they feel the whim. Everyone has a meaning behind their actions.

Some kind of motivation lies behind the cruel action of every man, no matter how random, or malicious it may seem to be. Hitler's hate for those of Jewish origin truly ignited when he was gracelessly shut out of his dream art school; one of the professors on the board that shut him down happened to be Jewish. This is admittedly an extreme example.

Why do you think as a child, anti-bullying assemblies always tried their hardest to pound into your head that bullies were also hurting?

It's an important thing to note and a very humanizing perspective to take toward the world. Taking a moment to stop in your daily routine and simply take it in, understand that the people around you are all leading lives, living in ruts very similar to yours.

Perhaps they aren't living in a rut at all; they may be incredibly satisfied with their situation, happy with their friends and their job and their spouse or significant other. They have dreams and aspirations and fears and hopes that plague them on a daily basis. Humans have so much depth to them. Humans are pack animals, social animals, and yet we fail to recognize that our peers are suffering and thriving in almost the exact same ways we are. We are living alongside them, even mirroring them, but we too often fail to recognize this because we are so focused on our own problems. This is the folly of the selfish man.

Other people suggest that we are bound to be good. In this view, no matter what heinous act we commit or what crime we are found guilty of or admit to, we will always be drawn back to good.

We live and breathe in a way no other creature on earth could ever hope to fathom. And yet, because we are so sentient and so inherently alive, we are chaotic by nature. We are not nearly simple enough to stick to either "good" or to "evil." We may find ourselves crossing into both often, and usually swerve around somewhere in the middle while we exist chaotically. We often live in the chaos that masquerades as peace and order.

There is a fatal flaw to the unanswerable question of whether or not humans are good or evil. Since we are so radically neither good nor evil, but retain the opportunity to be either, we will likely always end up somewhere in the middle. The problem with this perspective is that the question assumes that every person on earth has the exact same definitions for "good" and "evil.". Although it's a nice idea, it's ultimately not reality to expect cultures worldwide to always agree. So, humans are left with varying degrees for understanding how a scale of good and evil might operate in reality.

The debate on "good" versus "bad," or whether it's even a valid discussion to have in the first place, depends on the person asking the question. The real things that should be discussed by those looking to sharpen their skills in psychoanalysis are things that can be proven factually.

Although that subject sounds like quite a heavy one for a simple book about reading people and their body language, understanding what ties us all together as people shines a sharp, bright light on how to better understand and read people. The reality of reading people is simple when it comes to better understanding our common bonds. Although our differences are often massively dividing, our similarities far outweigh them.

Take, for instance, someone you know, a colleague or a friend of a friend, with whom you simply can't seem to get along. Something about them just feels off, although you can't quite figure out why. And yet, you steer clear of them anyway.

This may be because you're looking at your own personal differences from them. Try paying attention to the positive qualities of that person. In romantic relationships the difference between being in love and falling out of love with someone is how close of attention you pay to their positive qualities. When you fall out of love with someone you once thought you were inseparable from, it's likely because you've stopped taking the time to recognize all the good they do. You're so used to the good, that the bad becomes less noticeable. It is much the same in non-romantic relationships. We must consider consciously looking for the good in other people instead of automatically expecting the worst.

To maintain a better, or at least a more stable relationship with that person, you have to be able to do the work to recognize your similarities to them. Notice your heights or any similar traits you might have, whether they have freckles in the same spot or the same strange way you play with your food. These things may seem as though they will never matter in the grand scheme of things, but things like this are what build friendships and relationships. This logic can also be applied to help what may have otherwise been a failing or failed marriage.

You are not so different from one another after all. In fact, we're much more similar than we may think. We have the ability to notice any body language and internally interpret it without even realizing that we have done so. An interesting tidbit about body language: when we are with someone, we will instinctually try to replicate their body language and posture. This effect is called "mirroring," and it's what helps us better relate to the people we find ourselves among. It's a kind of built in friend-making device. We are bound to like people we find similar to us. As pack animals we would want to portray ourselves as being similar to the crowd we're in so that we can feel more accepted by that group; it makes sense to want to fit in, even from a primal perspective.

Which brings us to another of the darker aspects of human motivation and behavior: the sheer desperation to feel wanted and part of a group.

In part, desperation to be part of a particular group likely stems in part from modern society's hunger for to fulfill idealized and impractical dreams provided to us through various media sources. The concept of a "perfect life" has been so deeply ingrained into us that it may have been a driving force behind some people's ardent addiction to the feeling of automatic inclusion. It's almost as if we've come full circle, and have in some ways reverted back to that basic and primal need for the feeling of camaraderie.

Let's face it, belonging feels really, really good. The feeling of perfect togetherness is a desirable benefit of life. People who care for each other can all working toward a common goal and helping each other. It may not always look like what we expect, and it may take more work than we anticipate but improvements are possible.

That realization of a situation can be crushing to some young idealists. Reality can be enough of a blow to turn what were once hopeful and shining optimists into harsh and loathing cynics. The understanding that not everyone always finds a happy ending is sometimes too much for some people to take.

Understanding ourselves internally is possible. It is possible for us to gain perspective and use that information to help us draw out a better "self." Idealistic situations and perfect endings require a certain amount of luck along with them. Luck can sometimes look a lot like hard work. We do not have to discover everything all at once either. Producing lifelong outcomes will take time.

Desperation and cynicism regarding a goal that isn't satisfied can show the crazed lengths people will go to achieve their own desires. This is incredibly selfish, you might note, and you'd be right. You also might think to yourself that this is the image of a bad person. Is your version of "bad" the same as the person experiencing the negative situation that you are viewing as an outsider?

Selfishness is an inherently human trait. Without the sentience and the drive to achieve things you want, you would never get anywhere in life, although you wouldn't be selfish. We too often have a preconception about selfishness that the people that exhibit it are bad. This is also a false pretense.

We have this preconception because when we think of someone who is selfish, we often think of someone committing a heinous crime, or using the people around them for their own sick and cruel purposes. In reality, we are all selfish every day of our lives. We seem to have a particularly hard time accepting our own selfishness.

Maybe that is because of this "selfish equals evil" concept that we have buried in our brains. We are all selfish. Selfishness does not typically present itself in the form of a cruel and heartless boss who disposes of workers like yesterday's garbage. No, selfishness presents itself in small daily choices as well as impactful life choices. Selfishness can say, "I am going to put on my rescue mask first so that I can effectively help you." It can say, "I want the biggest piece of pizza. so I can share it with someone next to me."

Selfishness can present itself in ways that may be confusing to those who are not the one making the choice causing the action of selfishness.

Selfishness rears its not-so-ugly head in mundane and harmless forms, but it is still very much selfishness. It's prioritizing yourself over anything else, sometimes simply because the whim strikes you. Usually, although we may perceive it as such, this isn't actually such a bad thing. It's something that's also been ingrained in us since we were Neanderthal creatures, stumbling around and screaming at fire and anything that might pose any kind of threat to us. Ever since those days, we've retained a sense of self-centeredness, making ourselves the first priority because, well, if we didn't, we probably would have been wiped out by some unknown force a very long time ago.

So, you see, that guilt you feel when you do a little something for yourself is really unwarranted. We may have been trained to feel bad about feeling human impulses because they are just that: impulses. They can be incredibly unique to each person's experience, something our society ironically likes to try and reject. Of course, we know quite well that removing the uniqueness from man erases his identity—something that perhaps these days, mankind already seems perpetuate.

Taking these and other things out of a person will essentially make them into a kind of emotional vegetable; someone stripped of individuality. Where we exactly draw the line between what is natural to mankind at an acceptable level and what is evil and inherently unacceptable, completely varies by person to person. Accepting that good and evil coexist is perhaps the most crucial part of taking a step back and looking at society as a whole entity.

To better understand the nature of people as a complete group, let's quickly dive through a crash course in sociology, the study of how people—and larger groups of people—come together to form a messy and simultaneously very neat and immaculate society. There are, for beginners in the subject, three sociological theories of approach, otherwise referred to as sociological paradigms:

- Structural Functionalism: This is, in short, the most basic theory, and the most widely accepted theory by optimistic people as you may see throughout your life. Structural functionalism basically notes that maybe the reason society is still standing at all is that it's necessary to maintain order so that we don't all fall into an apocalyptic type of chaos. It dictates that society works a bit like a particularly well-oiled machine. It only hiccups every now and then, as most every machine does, and different parts of society, i.e. different groups, will all inevitably join together to create this machine. It also dictates that every institution that societies have in place, like schools, serve both an obvious purpose— what they were constructed for—and a latent purpose—one that only arose in the institution after it was built and put into practice, something that only occurs as an aftereffect.

Social Conflict Theory: This theory has become a bit more popular over time and was originally proposed by famed sociologist and philosopher—and better-known communist— Karl Marx. Social conflict theory basically just states that really, the only reason society is still together in one piece at all is that the world is, in a sense, one massive colosseum of groups of all backgrounds fighting either to keep their power or to take the power of someone else. Marx essentially envisioned the world and its various societies as different fighting rings where all the marginalized groups of the world fought the higher up more privileged groups. Given that we are currently living in a time of fairly evident racial conflict—it makes sense that this theory, in particular, took hold. It antagonizes the theory of the well-oiled machine, in a way. It takes the idea that we are all bound to work in harmony and throws it out the window, instead of shining the light on all the constant conflict and bloodshed that goes on in the world. Really, if we are meant to be a well-oiled machine, and that machine is supposedly working fairly well most all of the time, then what would you call our current time? How would you even begin to try and explain the hate and the violence and the atrocities that occur every day right under the top layer of that machine?

• Symbolic interactionism: This is the theory that operates completely separately of the other prior two, for the most part. Developed at a later time, the theory of symbolic interactionism focused less on the big picture of society, large groups interacting, and focused more on the micro-interactions of the world, how one individual treats another one person. This theory proposed an idea that doesn't rely on the largeness of a group or the scale of society to explain itself. The theory notes, to summarize it, that there are no absolute truths in the world. That, to make any sense of anything on earth, we have to individually break apart and come up with our own meaning to everything that we see. Raw facts do next to nothing to explain the majority of the world's happenings. It explains less about the world than assumptions without any facts at all. Perhaps this is why so many people act the way they do, making baseless assumptions based on hearsay and no actual facts that they've learned from any reputable sources. However, to understand those raw facts, we have to interact on an individual level and come to an understanding of what that certain fact actually indicates for us. This is why, in some societies, the hand symbol for "O.K." is actually an incredibly rude gesture. It's also the reason we all interpret the Rorschach inkblot test very differently from one another. For example, we all agree that a handshake symbolizes something very basic—a greeting. A handshake only indicates this because the overwhelming majority of society dictates it to be that way. We understand as raising only the middle finger at someone as being incredibly offensive and rude because, for the most part, we all agree that this is simply what that gesture means. Few people understand the original meanings behind the gestures that humans sometimes use to convey meaning. The meaning, or rather the connotation, of something has to have reached a conclusion between many different people so that the gesture, word, symbol, phrase, etc., can become a universally recognized entity throughout that society in particular.

All of these sociological paradigms come together to, essentially, show us one nearly undeniable truth about us, about the world, and about sociologists most of all:

We are absolutely desperate to understand ourselves, to the point of throwing out everything we may have been taught during childhood and later in adulthood purely for the sake of discovering the "correct" truth.

As we briefly touched on in the very beginning of this book, most humans have some kind of primal urge, a desire, or a need to know things. We noted that it was more than likely that this need was based on the satisfaction of understanding ourselves which, on its own, is certainly not a harmful, selfish, or malicious trait. If anything, it's more of a virtue than it is a vice or anything else. Many people identify with this endless quest for the ultimate comprehension of everything that can be known, and with that search for knowledge camaraderie brings man together.

We haven't yet touched on another root of this intense need to understand. Sometimes, it's not so much the comprehension that satisfies us, but the knowledge that we're irrevocably correct over others is what satisfies us.

Because we, as humans are, especially in a more modern society, increasingly self-conscious and insecure with our abilities, we are constantly struggling to fulfill the gaps in confidence that have been carelessly left unfilled by the people around us, our guardians, and ourselves. By filling in these gaps, we're satisfying one of our most deeply seated needs as humans: the need and the craving for self-validation. This need drives us, not only toward knowledge, but through other alleys for achieving our goals. This may be through servicing others for praise and validation, or like Emmett who we discussed earlier, emotionally inducing a cycle of verbal and emotional affection so that you can profit off of the cycle for yourself. A little selfish, no?

When we do go down the alley of seeking out gaps in our knowledge through gaining intelligence, it often has some positive byproduct whether you plan to use it to validate yourself or not. Even if you only search into something to prove a rival wrong or win a debate, you'll still end up notably more educated on the subject than when you started. If the primary function of this venture is to prove someone wrong or to try and hold some kind of power over someone—then the venture, obviously, is kind of fruitless, as it will only leave you feeling unfulfilled in the end. This kind of temporary power is the equivalent of a very short rush of dopamine a coffee cubes that you may find next to a checkout register. Yet the latent function, which is that you became educated on the subject you were learning more about, actually turned out to be more powerful and effective than the obvious function was.

The power of all three of those sociological paradigms can and will affect you on a daily basis, likely for the rest of your life. It likely already has affected your life every day up until this point. Not only this, but the darker aspects of human behavior have also likely been affecting you and your life interactions, both directly and independently. But, don't forget to avoid falling into cynicism. Let's operate from here on out under the assumption that, humans are neither good nor bad, not evil or righteous. We are natural creatures all interacting with each other at all times, trying to get by in our own hopes, dreams, and agendas. Let's use this mode of thinking from here on out to better streamline the information in the rest of this book. Because, as you know by now, everything you interpret from this book is completely up to you, and it's up to how you look at humans.

Chapter Six: Intelligence

Our next topic when it comes to understanding people and being able to better analyze, comes in the form of comprehending people before you can read between the lines, so to speak.

There are many different kinds of intelligence, of course. There's tactile intelligence for those who learn from using their hands. There's academic intelligence, or "book smarts." We can have musical intelligence, analytical intelligence, street smarts, and the list can go on and on forever and ever. To cut it short, there's one kind of intelligence that many of those who want to be able to psychoanalyze people more effectively lack, or at least have trouble wanting to learn: emotional intelligence.

Emotional intelligence is the collective experience by one person wherein they can relate to another person's struggles and feelings, be able to empathize with them, and therefore be equipped to console them if the need arises. That's a fairly all-encompassing definition, and it's the one we'll use in this text. To apply this concept, someone who is emotionally intelligent can easily get a grasp on the feelings of another person when they are upset, understand why they feel that way, and be able to try and make them feel better. They will be able to understand or figure out why that person is upset to begin with, and where they're coming from with those emotions. Someone who is emotionally unintelligent, to use the other side of that spectrum, can talk to someone about their feelings, but it will always be significantly harder for them to really understand the other person's feelings and thoughts—at least, the ones that don't fit their own connotation of what is "rational." People who suffer from an antisocial personality disorder, or those with sociopathic and psychopathic tendencies, for example, have an incredibly low emotional IQ, also known as an EQ.

Of course, some people were born with a lower tendency toward empathic behavior. This doesn't make them a mean or cold person, and it isn't particularly something within that person's control. However, your EQ is a trait that is in no way static. No matter what your EQ is right now, it is more than likely subject to change, perhaps in the near future.

Emotional intelligence is one of humanity's greatest attributes, many psychologists say. Because we are able to empathize like very few other animals can, we possess the ability to be supportive of one another instead of passively waiting for our luck to turn around so we can get out of a depressive state or any emotional stupor. It's because we are able to consciously make changes as opposed to leaving our emotional state up to fate. We also have the power to take our fate into our own hands as we help ourselves and others. We have this power to do, really, whatever we want. The only thing stopping you from living your life in the way you most feel comfortable with is the pressure to fulfill your expected role in society and the stress that comes with the thought of not falling perfectly into line with your peers and with the rest of society. Knowing this, how can we relate emotional intelligence with analyzing others?

Being able to empathize with others may actually be a great skill for someone who can analyze those around himself or herself. Someone who analyzes others in a cold, manipulative, and cynical manner will ultimately fall short of someone who is warm and empathetic toward those they want to understand. The point of psychoanalysis is not quite always to analyze the person. It's often to understand them instead. These may sound like synonyms, and in the sense of denotation they are, but the connotation of each is very different. To analyze is to put science to them and any situations surrounding you and them, you could say. While science and math may not require a lot in the way of empathy or personality requirements, language arts can be very different because they demand the student to analyze something with a certain about of subjectivity. Language arts involves understanding the parameters in which individuals communicate with one another. Building language arts skills does require a certain amount of empathy and understanding for the way other writers and communicators interact within their respective formats. Better understanding the insights of others helps us better understand ourselves and helps us better understand what it is that we were trying to analyze in the first place. This very same logic can effectively be applied to all different kinds of people. When you look at someone with more of a cold or analytical stance, you see only a certain layer of them. Someone who looks at a person through a purely analytical gaze will very likely see a bad person, plain and simple. This kind of stance toward people is effective and efficient but is also very cut and dry. Thinking this way limits the way you tend to perceive others and only lets you understand them in a way that conforms to pure, cold analysis.

Looking at that same person with a sense of empathy, on the other hand, can far widen your horizons in the sense of how you perceive that individual. While as a cold, often cynical analyst, you may see someone who has done wrong things or is often selfish as a bad person. People may try and claim to be unaffected by bias. Viewing people in this kind of light will not ever drive you to be more objective, it will only drive you toward negativity. All humans have at least some natural bias—it's unavoidable. Being aware of the bias will do more to better your sense of objective perspective than acting like you have no bias in the first place. Someone who is a little more subjective, a little more emotional in the way they view people around them, will understand that there are hidden motivations toward selfishness. Empathetic individuals will likely understand that the person near them is three-dimensional, a creature capable of many things and a person who has many facets to their personality.

Knowing and processing that every person around you is a three-dimensional person will ultimately offer you a helpful perspective as you interact with others, not just become better at understanding people. The categories that we sometimes automatically put people into may result from a pessimistic tendency for which we are not even aware we retain.

Many people struggle with their empathy, however. Because some people were born with fairly low empathetic tendencies, they may struggle to connect to others. Others suffer from anxiety or other things which prevent them from being able to interact as proficiently as some of their peers may be able to do. This may seem like a massive roadblock on the way to unlocking your secret knack for analyzing people, but it's an overwhelmingly common obstacle that most people will face at some point in their lifetime. If they don't struggle with being able to connect, they may find they're unable to disconnect from people, a separate problem which is all its own. Two sides of the same coin, but these concepts show opposing examples of a problem that we may each face at some point in our life. This may especially become more prevalent now as younger generations seem to struggle with connecting face to face with their peers. Now that we are faced with this issue, it's time to figure out how to properly overcome it for the sake of the coming generations. These are some things, in particular, to keep in mind when you face this kind of issue:

• We will seldom encounter an effective overnight fix for our problems. Worthwhile matters often require our time and devotion. No matter what society may try to sell you, there is usually not a quick fix for our problems. There is no pill to slim down perfectly in one week, no workout regime to make you look like a bodybuilder before this Friday's date, and there is no self-help book that will cure your depression or reverse your traumas. You have to be active and face your concerns, ailments, and potential problems. You have to be the one to spearhead the cause for your own improvements. It has to be you, and you alone, at first who seeks to better yourself at any cost, no matter what it takes. Trying to cheat your way through life will only end in you remaining back at square one. There are people around you and resources to help and support you, but you have to take that first and most difficult step into the unknown.

• Practice makes perfect, no matter what. As you practice analyzing people, opening up to people, and responding to people opening up to you, you will not only improve as a friend and significant other, but you will also be able to better understand the basics when it comes to psychoanalysis. Whether that be taking a deeper look at yourself or discarding any personality quizzes for the real you, these things will accumulate around your growing sense of emotional intelligence and ability to put it to good use in the real world.

• What is currently holding you back does not now and will never define you. Whether it is anxiety, stress, or decreased empathy, the things you face now may only affect you for a certain period of time. The exact length of that period of time depends entirely on how you face it, seek to correct it or at least better it, and move forward from it. The period will be much longer if you procrastinate on bettering yourself, and the period will be much shorter if you are proactive in correcting what you think needs improvement in yourself.

• Do not blame anyone. Often, as humans, we may have a bad habit of placing blame either on others, on ourselves, or on the world in general when we can find no one else in particular. When you find yourself point a finger at others, remember the blaming of others will not help you to resolve the issue you're facing. Blaming others may not even bring you temporary satisfaction. In addition, blaming yourself for inadequacies can be a fruitless attempt at punishing yourself. So, focus all the energy that would otherwise go into blaming someone or yourself, and channel it into being productive in bettering yourself and your situation. This will prove much more fruitful and much more worth your time. Those around you may also see the progress you make and be more willing to help you.

• Learning about yourself is hard, and sometimes grueling. It requires a genuine amount of hard work and persistence, and there are times when you will falter. It's ok, and it's normal to feel like you may be failing. The point of taking a path to better yourself is not to continue on in one constant, straight line until you cross the metaphorical finish line. Self-improvement is one of those things where the journey is often more fulfilling than the destination. Of course, you should be satisfied when you deem yourself finished for the time being. You should feel proud that you were able to do all of the things you did and still continue on regardless. Keep in mind that improvement is not often quick in coming, and it is not by any means easy or linear. You will have good days when you feel as though you could touch that finish line. There will be days where you feel as though that finish line couldn't possibly be further out of your reach as it drifts further and further away with each passing moment. The idea is for you to have enough faith in yourself and in those around you that you can keep going. Know that you can cross that finish line just like everyone else around you seeking to better themselves. Find comfort in the fact that most of the world is trying to be better in some way right about now.

• Your support system is important. While a fighter can hardly win without the necessary training and fighting spirit to do so, the fighter's morale wouldn't be nearly as stable if not for their fans and their support cheering in their corner of the ring. The same goes for any endeavor you go on, including self-improvement. Your support system, whether it be composed of your friends, your family, or any other loved ones, is there to support you and help you in any way they can. This is where practicing the vocalization of your feelings comes into play. The people in your corner of the ring can't help you very well if you're unwilling to tell them why you're struggling. Unless you properly communicate with them, you're going to feel as if you don't have a support system at all, and it may even feel as if they've turned their backs on you sometimes. Don't be afraid to voice any concerns you have; beefing up your confidence, with the help of your support system and loved ones, is the first step toward organically growing your own skills and your own confidence. You should never be afraid to try and win because your supporters will be there on your bad days when you fail or lose. Even then, that loss is only temporary.

Understanding a little bit better how emotional intelligence, or EQ, factors into psychoanalysis means also taking a bit of a glimpse into what separates individuals who try to analyze in a harsh or cold manner from those who seek to better understand the people they are reading. Looking below the surface of what is readable about others at a glance can have an impact on how we train ourselves to respond to others. The latter of those individuals will go on to be significantly better listeners and more persuasive as well. Growing skills for empathetic living can help us have a better grasp on what makes other people frustrated and what might please them or win them over in an argument.

Additionally, those who can empathize with the people will be able to make faster connections much easier. What this means is that much of human behavior draws back to a certain handful of causes, most of which are rooted in childhood. These things aren't always acting as a secret villain behind a person's erratic or otherwise strange behavior. Yet, an educated guess as to that person's history, while also taking a look at why those things are so often the root cause of the massive majority of divergent behavior may be helpful. After all, since childhood causes seem to be the reality for so many people, what trend in society that can be linked to the surge of people acting the way they do? What does it all seem to say about our society as a whole, and is there any way to reduce or change it? In the next chapter, we'll dive a little deeper into the art of persuasion, and how psychoanalysis factors heavily into winning an argument or running a political campaign.

Chapter Seven: To Convince the Mind

The art of persuading others, especially in a world in which words can travel quickly through communities, is to essentially control the majority of the people in some situations. This is why being able to articulate your needs and intentions is such a important trait to have as a politician or in a similar position of power. Individuals in these different positions of power often have an ability to win over other people and persuade them to consider their side of an argument. They often end up remaining in that powerful position for as long as they're able to as they continue working with the concepts they believe are good and beneficial for their respective societies. Truly, in any kind of democracy where the citizens are left to decide their own leaders, it's the power of the spoken word that wins elections and polls nationwide.

Now, the only question left is this: how easy is it—or rather, how long will it take—to learn how to influence people, to bend them to a certain party's will? Really, it's not nearly as difficult as many people might make it out to be. Of course, there are some people who are going to have a previously acquired affinity for persuading others. There are some who will always naturally find it easy to convince others who is right and who is wrong. This is normal, and maybe one of these people is you. If this is the case, be thankful for your talent, but know that no talent will ever be able to match a skill acquired through long periods of practice and honing.

If you aren't someone with a naturally born gift for persuasion or someone who happened to be the star of your high school's debate team, don't worry! Things come easier the more you focus and practice—and the spoken word is no exception.

Something to be noted, before we go further into discussing the uses and benefits of being able to persuade others efficiently, is that the line between persuasion and manipulation is often very thin and blurry. Understanding the difference between persuading someone for a good purpose and manipulating someone to do something for selfish or malicious reasons means understanding the difference between a creative communicator and a potentially dangerous individual. Although we all subconsciously manipulate others in some way or another, intentionally going out of your way to do it to someone for your own benefit is morally frowned upon by society. The act of forcefully bending someone to your will is an act of someone who doesn't have the courage to either do what they want to be done for themselves or is possibly too cowardly to simply ask the person for what is needed. If you intend to do anything taught in this book with malicious intent or in order to cause discord in someone else's life, this book is not for you. That rule applies to everything taught in this book, and that very much includes persuasion vs. manipulation, which will be discussed further in the next chapter.

Now, the first step to learning how to better persuade others is learning how to better articulate your own needs, desires, and views. Scarcely will anyone ever be properly persuaded or convinced by someone who doesn't even sound confident in their own ideas.

Often, this is what people trying to learn how to convince people and be more persuasive have the most problems with as they learn to speak in front of a crowd. This is often because confidence is incredibly difficult to develop without a strong support system. It's not something to be honed over a few weeks or something that can be corrected with a small amount of self-awareness, like verbal articulation. No, confidence is something that grows more slowly than almost anything else, something that needs the fostering of many days over months and, sometimes over years. Growing that confidence is undeniably difficult for everyone, no matter what their background or their past and present circumstances. The trial of taking that kind of an inner journey is always made especially difficult for those who suffer from larger than average amounts of anxiety or have other prominent sources of stress. Noting these difficulties shouldn't ever be made into a reason to excuse your refusal to gain more confidence. Though there are always roadblocks in your way, the existence of these obstacles is no real reason to refuse help from others and remain static. If you don't choose to let yourself evolve both as a psychoanalyst and as a person, it's more than likely that you'll always be left far behind by your peers who are more than willing to evolve when you are not.

As we discussed earlier, many people who want to gain more confidence but don't have the time or the mental fortitude to keep up the consistency of working on self-love and self-care and everything else that goes into organically nurturing confidence simply fake it. This kind of attitude, the "fake it until you make it" mindset can be detrimental in the long run if you never learn to separate the façade from reality, As long as you're willing to eventually let go of the façade and embrace the real confidence that has grown behind it, this kind of thinking can actually be very helpful, depending on the person and on the context under which they adopt that mindset.

The way this kind of mindset actually works is by taking advantage of the placebo effect. This placebo effect relies on the fact that our brain will believe anything we tell it, essentially. For example, two groups of people may be told they are going to be testing a new over-the-counter pill for congestion. One group is given a pill with a decongestant effect, and the other group is given an identical sugar pill that looks, tastes, and feels identical in texture to the real pill. Both groups of people report feeling nearly identical reactions, feeling decongested and overall better. Both groups may report being happy with the results. This happens because the brain of the sugar pill group was convinced by those conducting the experiment that the pill they were taking contained a decongestant, and therefore it simulated a decongestant effect of its own as a reaction. Of course, the placebo effect may have a slightly less powerful effect than what happens for a group that is actually receiving a foreign chemical entity. The point is that the "mind over matter" concept not only has notable a scientific basis, but it can also be applied practically to the extent that this placebo effect can be used to convince people that the effect will be positive, or at least that there will be some kind of benefit. This placebo effect factors into the "fake it until you make it" method heavily, because the reason we feel more confident almost immediately once we put this method into use in our lives, is because we've effectively convinced the brain that we are now notably more confident than we were prior to experiencing that coping mechanism. As a reaction, the brain releases hormones to aid in this process, making us genuinely more confident. So, believing that you are more confident will, to a certain extent, actually make you more confident, effective immediately.

Most people you encounter who have a lot of confidence have probably faked it at some point or another and may or may not be faking it at that very moment at which you observe them. It's not necessarily a bad thing at all, or anything anyone should be ashamed of using as a kind of emotional crutch or coping mechanism. We all fake something to a certain extent. Faking anything well enough to fool the brain even for a period of time is more than enough to actually feel the effects. This is sometimes why people report certain home remedies work, even though logically they shouldn't, and most of them don't work on those who are skeptic of their abilities. The people using them and putting them into effect are the people who actually believe in their abilities and believe that they will feel better or be healed because of what ails them. Therefore, they experience those exact effects, in part, because of their own thinking. On the other hand, skeptics believe they will not experience a change, and therefore they often do not experience the relief or effect that believers in the home remedy do. This kind of thinking affects us in almost every portion of our lives, and it shouldn't be cast off as some kind of phony possibility. It may be perceived that everyone who believes in home remedies is being faked out by one massive story in a hidden world of marketing all over the world. However, personal research must be done to ensure that each situation involves truth for each potential placebo situation. Some home remedies do have a history that tells us why they do or do not work. Other remedies currently have less scientific study material to back them up properly. How well the guidelines for a home remedy are followed also play a role in how well they work for each person seeking their benefits. The placebo effect is very real and will affect you undoubtedly at some point in your life, even if you do not fully realize it.

Now that we've gone over ways you can actually attain an increased level of confidence, practice public speaking! It may seem incredibly unnecessary to most people to practice this kind of thing with any regularity. However, doing this will make you more confident in your abilities as a speaker in your daily conversations, boosting both your articulation skills and your confidence. See, things like this influence each other the more you practice each one of them. No matter how reminiscent of grade school it might seem, practice speaking on a subject that you care about, even if it is only to peers or to other loved ones. This will help you increase your persuasion abilities as well as your group speaking skills. One of the many keys to becoming better at the art of persuasion is being able to talk passionately. If someone sees that you care about what you're discussing, they're more likely to be drawn into whatever it is you are arguing to achieve or develop. Doing this alone won't win many people over in the end but making sure that you have an attentive audience is the first step to winning your debate.

Now, the next most important part of being able to persuade others is actually being able to analyze your audience. Consider what might be influencing your audience to listen to your argument. What kinds of people might agree with you? Depending on the answer to that question, be sure to cater specifically to that audience in particular. Doing this will better your chances of getting more people on your side. When thinking about what kinds of people you may be pandering or catering toward during your argument, consider some of these general questions:

> • What is the exact age range of the audience you're trying to pander? Depending on the answer to this question, you can better understand how to appeal to that specific audience. A younger audience will often be more drawn to an argument with a lot of passion and a certain sense of renewal: the young overtaking the old, the new way overtaking any classic concepts. An older audience will want to listen to a more steadfast debater, someone who is calm and collected in their argument but still has the overwhelming ability to call the listener to action. An older audience tends to be more partial to a sense of nostalgia. Take, for example, President Donald Trump. His presidential campaign featured the slogan "Make America Great Again!" This slogan marketed toward an older audience, but the slogan directed itself toward the kind of audience who is more susceptible to both a kind of call to action, and an audience who finds themselves more drawn to that nostalgia for the "America" they grew up in years ago. Older audiences also generally like to be told that their reasons and their beliefs in things are undeniably correct—as most people do, young and old.

• Consider the sex of your audience as well. This will often majorly affect how you present your argument. Generalizing is tricky when it comes to massive groups, but it's still important to distinguish what you can when considering to what kind of people you are going to market yourself or your conversation points. In particular, consider how feminine or how masculine your target audience will be. This sometimes matters even more than whether the majority of your actual audience is actually male or female. A hyper-feminine group of women may have different interests than a group of women seeking to spend their time in the outdoors with little access to amenities. Keep in mind that catering to a particular sex is different than being sexist, and where you draw the line will determine your fate and your potential popularity with your audience. Typically, women want to feel empowered by whoever they invest their time or energy into regularly. They want to feel like an equal because traditionally they may have been made to feel as if they have to make up for something they intrinsically lack when stacked up against their male counterparts. On the flip side of that spectrum, men tend to not to look for something incredibly thought-provoking or philosophical. Men often look for passion and energy in the physical sense more than the emotional sense, as opposed to their female peers. Keeping this in mind, be careful how far into each stereotype you cross.

Consider the background of the majority of your audience. Whether this is race, environment, political leaning, religion and spirituality or a lack thereof, or a multitude of other factors. All of these factors will play a large role in how you communicate with them in order to persuade them and market your points to that audience. An audience that is particularly spiritual or religious will likely have an appreciation for a speaker that works those elements into their argument or appeal to the audience. An audience whose majority is marginalized because of race, religion, sexual orientation, or anything else that may cause that audience to feel as if they have less of a public voice than some of their peers will feel an attachment to a speaker whose points recognize their concerns in life. Potential listeners will be more likely to pay attention if they observe that the speaker is willing to appeal to them as individuals who feel marginalized or buried beneath the voices of those around them who too often are given a disproportionately loud voice by comparison. Walking the line between speaking up for marginalized groups and ignoring the pleas of the majority, who may or may not actually make up a part of your particular audience, is difficult. Even when the majority is not part of your audience, they are still affected by your points and your argument. Angering the majority will both decrease the chances of your audience growing and will increase the negative impression you leave on the audience of the other party—if there is another party or parties. Additionally, it is not always in the best interest of the group that you are speaking to actually advocate for them unless you are someone either in that particular demographic or someone who has extensive knowledge on it to the point where you are educated enough to speak on it. An advocate for transgender people will likely not be able to speak on their prejudice as well or as powerfully as an actual transgender person would be able to in some situations. Keep this in mind when advocating. Trying too hard to be an ally may actually result in the opposite effect. Also, consider any other possible bonding points among the majority of the members of your audience. Whether it be the time period in which they were born or an experience that bonds together most of the people you happen to be catering to, it's the experiences that people coincidentally tend to share that are sometimes also the strongest. Interaction with your audience is often understood as one of the hidden treasures of public speaking and debate and argument. This is often the secret to the seemingly effortless talent that comes from many of the most powerful, influential, and well-liked public speakers. What many people in positions of power who must address the public draw upon as they give a speech is the camaraderie that comes with being human. This feeling of togetherness and unity is often the driving force of the most powerful speakers.

It is the majority of these factors combined with other topic-specific matters that can play a role in what kind of audience you will want to recognize. You will need to assess these factors together as they will ultimately have the heaviest hand in determining how successful you turn out to be in improving your ability to communicate to large and small groups. In addition to this, always remember that what sells your points more than actually being accurate, is confidence. It sounds ridiculous—and more so than that, it sounds unjust—but it's true, People who are looking for a speaker or someone in a position of power are usually not so much looking for someone who has their facts straight, but simply someone who can convince a crowd that if they lean in their favor, they'll be on the right side of history. To convince the mind of only one person can be to cause a chain reaction which shifts the popular opinion of an entire group. The facts will never be what actually sells your point, as terrible as that may sound. No, it will never be the correctness of your position or the accuracy of your points that get people to understand you and support you. Instead, it's confidence that convinces people. If someone stands on a stage and delivers a speech that is totally correct but given by someone who severely lacks confidence, the chances of them winning a majority are slim to none at best. But, someone who stands up and gives a speech that is wrong, even to the extent of spreading harmful or dangerous misinformation but who delivers the speech with an air of confidence and certainty, one who knows how to be charismatic and approachable, will almost definitely win a popular vote every single time. Sure, that's insane!

Why would people actively want to vote for someone that's wrong? Think of who you would like to observe more in a program involving two speakers. The points and the argument are the exact same, given by two different people. The people are identical except that one of them is very shy, unconfident, and unsure of the points. The other has no idea whether they are actually correct or not but charges blindly forward anyway. They're charismatic, personable, and well-spoken.

You would more than likely choose the candidate who is more well-spoken and charming in the way they present themselves and the way they speak. Even though you were consciously aware that they were arguing identical points in the same way. The way the more confident person made you feel about their argument is what changed you toward their favor.

This is an example of how you can argue and debate effectively for the purpose of your intended goal. Genuinely how you present yourself in a public setting, can actually factor heavily into the art of psychoanalysis. Think for a moment on how you read people who are confident. Knowing that people are often already falsifying their confidence in many situations, may help you feel more comfortable navigating your own road to confidence and positive persuasion. For one thing, seeing people in positions of power speak confidently on a subject they might actually know very little to nothing at all about is a great example of this exact kind of persuasive person. Someone who is uneducated can still get ahead easily in a debate, argument, or really any other scenario in which an individual has to present their opinions or win over favor. This may be specifically true for the favor of large amounts of people they might not know personally. Simply analyzing the potential audience and catering to them in the way they conduct themselves, their tone of voice, content of conversation, and body language may win them the attention they seek. Understanding what an outstanding effect such a small and seemingly meaningless concept may have on our perception of a situation can help us change the outcome for the better. Knowledge, proper confidence, and audience awareness are important keys to unlocking our own abilities to do things for ourselves and others. Consciously, tricking our brains into believing something until we are fully equipped to do something more independently, can help us have the power to practice what we actually want to learn to do.

In this next chapter, we'll talk a bit more about the darker side of persuasion—manipulation. We'll also discuss how to draw the line between what is benevolent and malevolent with respect to when people use their skills for psychoanalysis to manipulate others.

Chapter Eight: Two-Sided Coin

The line between persuasion and manipulation is as thin as the side of a coin. The two forms of getting other people to understand the world a little bit differently according to our own views, actions, or desires. Flipping this coin is easy and can be done deliberately or in many cases, accidentally. Being wary of what lies on the other side of the coin can help you to stay out of a lot of moral trouble, as well as keep you from misusing your abilities of psychoanalysis.

On one side of this coin is persuasion, a relatively innocent form of manipulation. To persuade covertly is obviously usually frowned upon in society. However, persuading someone without their knowledge is usually not particularly easy. Persuasion is simply the art of using subtle things about people—their tone of voice, their exact wording, their posture, their body language, and a multitude of other small factors to garner their favor. People will often unconsciously take such information into their mental storehouses and allow it to influence their choices, family decisions, and goals for life. You may find yourself using this information to your advantage by promoting yourself or your situation as the best possible option compared to any competition. Of course, there are many ways that this information could be mistreated by people in a position to persuade. There are also bound to be many, many people who simply see fit to use unlawful or generally immoral practices when debating or arguing for a group's vote or favor. These facts aside, let's focus more on the darker side of this coin.

Manipulation, to take a closer and potentially colder, more cynical look at that very same coin, falls under the umbrella of what I was describing when I mentioned that people may attempt to persuade others covertly or without the viewers or otherwise participating person's permission or consent. This can lead to a lot of problematic behaviors and habits if not addressed properly. Of course, there are people who accidentally display these habits and behaviors and are generally not ill-intentioned in their efforts. However, someone who steals without knowing it ceases to be on the side of the law. Let's go a bit deeper into outlining the difference between persuasion and manipulation of others.

Take, as an example that you were at a party. There's someone who is dancing quite intimately next to you and tries to convince you to leave the party to come to their house. Neither of you is under the influence of alcohol and are both above the age of consent. The person may try to appeal to your sense of loneliness by telling you that they will be sure to make you comfortable and safe. This may be viewed as persuasion leaning on the edge of manipulation—the other party is trying to convince you by taking advantage of the information they've already picked up about you.

The same person might also try to convince you to come home with them from the party by pointing out that you are lonely, in great need of comfort, and unable to proceed on your own for a reason that they have observed about you. Deception is also a key factor in manipulation. These are ways that manipulation, emotional manipulation to be more specific, is different than persuasion. Also known as "gaslighting" in the context of a potentially abusive or neglectful romantic relationship, this kind of manipulation involves using information that the person already has or has guessed about you, and they actively use that information to guilt you into doing what they want you to do. They are likely doing this because they are not particularly well spoken and see no other way to get you to bend to their wants or desires. So, persuasion and manipulation are two sides of the same metaphorical coin which are often intertwined, but still very distinct and separate ways to try and win over a person.

Something else to be considered when talking about the distinctions between persuasion and manipulation is how that hypothetical person may react if you reject their offer. The person who simply tried to persuade you might be a adamant about the situation but will usually overall give up when you flatly decline. He or she may be disgruntled or disappointed but will usually drop the offer afterward. Someone who opened with trying to manipulate you using guilt likely will have a much harder time being rejected. This kind of person will more than likely refuse to take "no" for an answer, and will often keep pushing you, sometimes until the situation turns potentially dangerous. This is a kind of person you should generally try to avoid at all costs. Should you encounter them in a public setting , you should make sure you have your cellphone or someone else who could help you out of a potentially harmful scenario. Even though this is only a contingency and is in no way guaranteed, the safety of everyone that could be in contact with people like this is the top priority. Also, it should be noted that when someone tries to persuade you, especially in the situation of a party as described in the example, it's usually not a matter of the person who tried to persuade you simply letting it go and walking away on the first try. Persuasion can turn ugly just as fast as someone who tries to manipulate or gaslight you but tend not to be as malevolent as someone who genuinely can't seem to find a way to try and convince you without being deceptive . Someone who at first tries to persuade you may be very adamant in their persuasion for some time. If those persuasive tactics do not work, things may quickly develop into a situation of manipulation through deceit, veiled partial truths, or personal information that you may not want shared. Again, this is only a contingency, but it's one that happens more than it should. Anyone who finds themselves in a scenario similar to this one, most often young women, should be aware of people of this type and be able to find a way to safely navigate the if a situation arises. Be prepared to call the proper authorities, get help from someone you genuinely trust, and remove yourself from the situation at once.

The difference, intrinsically, in the way persuaders and manipulators use their analytical skills for reading people actually rests in what they do with the information they are absorbing. They take in essentially the same information, but they don't really seem to use it in the exact same way. People who have more of an affinity for persuasion, using smooth talk and body language to assure and convince an audience, will tend to take in information about a person or people they are trying to persuade, and tailor their posture, voice, and exact words to that person or people by shifting their argument.

Someone who primarily manipulates others, however, is a bit different. Someone who has an affinity for manipulation will use the same information not to change their body language or tone of voice or word choice to reassure their audience, but perhaps to intimidate them. Usually, manipulators are or have the potential to be abusive individuals, emotionally and verbally or otherwise, so it's important to note the distinguishing factors of someone like this. A manipulator usually will not quite tailor themselves to the person with whom they are talking but will instead seek to guilt them or scare them into doing what the manipulator is asking of them.

However, certainly not every manipulator is like this. Not every person who wants to manipulate you or otherwise bend you to their will is the kind of manipulator who would so openly portray their plans to you. These parameters give you a guide for how to recognize the difference quickly so that you may respond in a safe and timely manner. Perhaps the most utterly terrifying kinds of manipulators are the kinds that live among us who seek control of our feelings. It may be that the scariest kind of manipulator is the kind who you don't even know is manipulating you.

This kind of manipulation also comes in the form of an abuser. Behind closed doors, they may be the spitting image of the kind of individual described in the party example. Behind closed doors, they may be a different kind of person entirely, or they may not. That all depends entirely on the person we're discussing. However, the kind of person I'm talking about now is the kind of person who manipulates you in a way that pins you against yourself. They may not physically pin you down in any way, but they seek to use your own situations against you. This kind of person is especially dangerous in that they are intelligent, clever, and malevolent enough to actively make you feel as if you must respond in the way they suggest. You may even feel as though you consciously recognize that person's actions are abusive or manipulative, but you fail to be able to convince yourself that you could ever confront them. They may have made you feel invalid in your feelings and in your thinking.

Although this kind of toxic dynamic is more often found in a relationship where a man is controlling, overbearing, and manipulative of a female spouse, the dynamic can be easily spotted in any kind of relationship, romantic or platonic. This kind of dynamic forms when the abuser or manipulator makes a consistent habit of aggressively putting down a partner and making them feel inadequate. It may be as if anything that comes out of their mouth is not only blatantly wrong but makes it an embarrassment for the person to even think about what is said. This kind of abuser will shroud their verbal and emotional abuse in affection and what they would call "love." They will intermittently shower their partner or spouse with lots of affection and physical validation and pleasure. It may be that more often showing that "love," they will put down, degrade, or otherwise shame their partner. This becomes a harmful and abusive cycle where the victim is too meek and too afraid of voicing their opinions to confront their abuser, let alone get up and leave. This cycle keeps victims of abuse locked into their relationships for months, years, and far too often for the rest of their lives.

Now, let's show how this is a relevant connection to psychoanalysis. One way that many victims of abusive relationships ending up finding a way out of that relationship is by breaking the cycle by force. There are many ways to do this—some victims find the power to break the cycle of verbal and psychological abuse before it wraps them up too tightly, cutting ties very early to the relationship. Even this can have negative and lasting effects, as manipulative individuals and abusers will often stalk their past partners to try and reconnect or restart the cycle of abuse. Most victims, unfortunately, aren't lucky enough to see the red flags before it's too late to duck out of the. Another large group of victims find strength by communicating via online forums where other survivors of abuse gather and support each other. Often, this positive—and often very new—force in a victim's life is at least enough to shake away some of the weight the abuser has left on them. It often will not result in permanently rendering the victim of abuse suddenly able to stand up and fight their abuser, but support like this is enough to give many fellow victims a fighting chance against the actions of their manipulators.

Sometimes victims who are trapped in a cycle of abuse are able to find added strength by giving their abuser a taste of his or her own medicine. They often do this by analyzing them in a way the abuser analyzed them in order to take advantage of what they had originally seen as "weak spots" in the emotional armor of their victim. Victims may notice patterns in their abuser's schedule and will be able use a time when they are gone or otherwise distracted to physically escape from them.

If you are in a dangerous situation with a dangerous individual or you are a spectator of such a dangerous situation, call the proper authorities immediately.

Note that manipulation is a prevalent aspect of psychoanalysis and not something that should be taken lightly. Manipulation of all kinds is also often viewed as simply another side of the coin in comparison to persuasion. The previous chapters will come together in the next, final two chapters to help you better understand how to combine all of the methods discussed and allow them to culminate in the best and most efficient ways to gain a better understanding of those around you.

Chapter Nine: The Science of Quick-Slicing

A common misconception about psychoanalysis is that is that it is similar to naturalistic observation or a case study, in that it must take place over the course of many months and often even years. This is simply not true. In all fairness, psychoanalysis is very much like naturalistic observation, but really only in the sense that it's a tool used by psychologists or people interested in behaviors of other people to gauge or test their theories about the world around them as well as to test the people within it.

It should be noted that the art of "quick slicing," or rapid cognition as we will refer to it for the rest of this book for simplicity's sake, is not a tool that's ideally suited for everyone. Some people will find that using rapid cognition to better understand their peers and to gain an insight into the world comes very naturally to them, and other people will struggle intensely with the subject matter. There's absolutely nothing wrong with having little or no desire to learn how to use and apply rapid cognition, The beauty in analyzing others with a soft science like behavioral psychology is that there is definitely a certain amount of discretion that goes into it. There's a certain extent to which you can really call all of the shots. Of course, there are certain guidelines and specific rules of thumb that are in your best interest to follow, but overall, it's up to you how to best use your abilities and any of the skills you may have learned while reading this book.

Put simply, rapid cognition is the process and the ability to unconsciously tap into information that you've picked up on from a person, place, or group of people in a very short amount of time.

For example, a study was done in which several college students were told to leave their dorms for twenty minutes in its most natural state—how they would normally leave it. Then, close friends of those students were given exactly five minutes to go into the dorm room and look around the room. They were never allowed to touch or otherwise interact with anything in the room, only to observe. After the five minutes were up, in came total strangers who had never met the college student to investigate on their own, for the same amount of time of five minutes. However, at the end of the study, it was found that when answering questions about the students' lifestyles and probable personality traits, the people who had never met the college students answered a profiling questions about the occupants almost identically to the answers given by the close friends of those very same students. This is a prime example of rapid cognition. Most humans have an innate sense of social and behavioral cues. A few small and seemingly irrelevant details about even a person's bedroom can indicate telling features about a person. Seeing a kind of "organized" mess can indicate that the owner of such a mess may actually be a semi-orderly thinking person even if the "organization" only makes sense to them, Someone with a mess that seems more careless may give an impression of being a scatterbrained, but creative person. Using small details that even we often don't know that we pick up on our own with our unconscious mind, it's rather easy to quickly and efficiently piece together an often fairly factual image of a person, even if we haven't met them or otherwise interacted with them. As you can see, even in a matter of minutes, we have the ability to understand the people around us with much more depth and clarity than we often give ourselves credit for having at our disposal.

The science behind rapid cognition is fairly simple. Our conscious brain, the part of our mind in which we store information that is prevalent and relatively short-term, keeps track of many things. It may easily reach a point of sensory overload, as the conscious mind can only truly focus its attention on one central concept at a time. The unconscious mind, however, which keeps track of our memories, our traumas, and our other long-term information, is much larger in terms of space available, and therefore there is a significantly lower chance that it can be overloaded with information and stimuli. However, because we so often do not feel the need to actively open up our subconscious mind, we often don't even recognize the immense power this part of our thoughts. Our unconscious brain isn't likely to be overloaded compared to the conscious mind simply because it can handle much more information at one time. After all, it is built to be a vault of sorts for information we don't need to keep on hand.

In addition to this overwhelming metaphorical size, our unconscious does not need to be actively thinking about something to be taking in information on it. In fact, most of the time, your unconscious is taking in massive amounts of information without you even knowing it. This is why people often experience a sensation of familiarity with things they should not have ever had any kind of contact with in the past. If we could hypothetically link our conscious and our unconscious minds together, we could effectively increase our general knowledge, our processing power, and many other mental processes exponentially. We would become much more intellectually advanced beings, as well as much more efficient ones. Keeping this in mind, rapid cognition is an ability that needs to be honed or sharpened with time. Rapid cognition is something less attributed to the innate and natural talent of some individuals. We can process information at a much faster rate and build estimated guesses because of it.

When you feel as though your gut is pulled in some specific direction, even though you don't feel much of a logical reason behind that "gut feeling" or instinctual feeling, it's actually your unconscious mind processing information that your conscious mind did not.

Rapid cognition relies heavily on that kind of gut instinct feeling, the generalization and "first impression" energy you feel from someone. Although for most of human history these kinds of assumptions were either considered something of supernatural descent or, something entirely inconclusive. We now have a better understanding of the human mind so that we may definitively say that we do have the processes in our unconscious mind to determine many things about someone just at a glance. Understanding this can be scary for some who are often judged by their physical features before their verbal or behavioral cues—e.g., someone with a very menacing posture or something about them physically that is negative and also out of their control. It should be noted that a large part of this "first impression" concept is mainly composed not of the physicality of someone, but instead of the body language and verbal, behavioral, and otherwise controllable aspects that are indicative of someone's personality. We as humans have a bad habit of taking a very long time to analyze someone. However, using rapid cognition, it's easy and plain to see that using large quantities of time to examine someone psychologically is simply unnecessary, unwarranted, and inefficient in the grand scheme of psychoanalysis.

Instead of wasting so much time performing such an in-depth search on someone, you can look at someone and their body language, tone of voice, and every other aspect of a person's posturing for less than a minute. With this miniscule amount of time compared to how much time we often take to examine someone in the very same way, we more often than not can form essentially the same estimations and educated guesses on the person or people we're analyzing—or at least, are trying to analyze at that moment. This is only because when you watch someone for five minutes versus thirty seconds, you're working with the very same base information on that person. The only difference is you've been given extra time to examine the nuances and very small details of the way that person behaves, along with that base information about their behavior. In reality, these tiny nuances are often an afterthought compared to that basis of understanding we know have on that individual. The things we understand about that individual—or rather, the large and more obvious clues about their behavior—are the metaphorical grand center of the strange compared to the smaller nuances that are swept to the side by comparison. Really, in the bigger picture of that person's behavior, these small details simply don't matter. The nuances that indicate what exactly might cause the individual to act the way they do is irrelevant when watching someone for interest and curiosity more than to find an actual answer. Whether or not someone is anxious because of past cases of abuse or simply because they're genetically prone to an anxiety disorder have to change the fact of them becoming your friend. What does matter is the way they hunch and curl in on themselves, the clearly unconfident and shy way they communicate toward others, and the way they seem to flinch away when spoken to harshly, among many other clues. When analyzing someone using the methods discussed in this book, you are not usually looking for those tiny and often unimportant details. You are looking for the big picture which will indicate a person's probable personality type. The reasoning behind that behavior, in particular, is an afterthought, something that can be tended to later when you have the proper time, the proper connection, and the proper energy.

These afterthoughts often aid us immensely in actually piecing together an entire story in respect to an individual and why they may act the way they do, their motivations, and often their past. However, when you first analyze a person, you want to cast your net wide, so to speak. It's much better and much easier not to spend a lot of energy on one aspect of a person's character or how they portray themselves. Rather shoot to spend minimal energy looking at a wide range of aspects of their persona, their body language, and their cadence and certain tics you might notice. There are other tics and various details you won't notice at first, and that's ok. Part of psychoanalysis is that you don't notice a lot of things that might turn out to be relevant until far after you've taken your first glance, stuck your first toe deep into the water. Rapid cognition in that sense can be compared to a method many artists use when they have an idea for work in which they create many "thumbnails." In this sense, "thumbnail" refers to a large number of incredibly messy and quick sketches that are made in rapid succession until the creator has a precise understanding of what their finished product may look like. This includes where they may want a subject to stand, in what position they should be placed, Some details and aspects of the background, the angle, the lighting, and many other details will have to be heavily considered before a finished work can be produced.

Similar to rapid cognition, when making thumbnails, an artist has to cast the net wide creatively, in that they have to pull ideas from every corner of their mind and throw them down on paper or canvas to see how it looks. In these thumbnails, the idea for a more formal and final creation can be produced. Similarly, some corporations and other business entities have adopted this way of thinking, by asking employees not a lot of time on one trial of a product, but rather to spend more of their time making many messy prototypes until they can make one that works most ideally for what they want specifically out of the product. This allows them not only to encourage productivity and creativity but also allows the workers to fail without punishment or ridicule. In the real world, we fail many times while making something or doing something before we succeed. What makes us succeed in the end is, in large part, the information and feedback we've received along the way. This rapid feedback system is exactly what many artists and businesses are trying to reproduce.

Going back to the aforementioned information about the mask legends of ancient Japan, wherein every person has three masks which they show to separate groups within their lives, it can be said that when you first try to analyze someone, you are not looking at their third mask, the one which they show only to the mirror, which represents their deepest and often darkest "self." No, instead we most often are looking at their very first mask, the mask which they show not only to themselves but to the entire world. This is their public mask, the character which is often a façade which they manufacture and are sure to only show to the public. In the unfinished and edited notes of the late sociologist G.H Mead, we hear more information about his theory of the self, in many ways his information correlates the with ancient Japan's understanding of the self. In the notes, Mead notes the existence two separate but bonded and coexisting "selves," called the "I" and the "Me."

The "I," says Mead, represents the way that an individual interacts with the self. It is the manifestation of how one person treats themselves and how they are likely to treat or mistreat the image they see in the mirror every day. The "me" on the other hand, is a much more fluid sense of self that is derived solely from social interaction. The "me" is the self that is produced based on the way most people you meet in life, and how they treat you or mistreat you. If most of the people who interact with you treat you very harshly or negatively—such as a child who grew up in an abusive, neglectful, or otherwise unhealthy home—your "me" will change accordingly, often either withdrawing and becoming an exceedingly untrusting and scared self or a self that is vicious and cruel, untrusting. The individual may unknowingly continue the cycle of abuse toward others as they seek to interact in ways that seem natural to them.

Our "me(s)" interact with one another and change each other on a daily basis, whether we touch with another person literally or otherwise. Our I(s) however, do not ever interact with someone else and are only affected by our me(s). If your "me" were to take a significant blow to the self-confidence or to the ego for some reason, your "I" would be affected, but only proportionately to how the "me" was affected. The "I" will never be as highly affected by interactions as the "me," but extreme social conditions that the "me" is placed under will sometimes indirectly interact with and change the "I" as well. This is often in a much less extreme way in proportion to the amount the "me" was infected by the stress or effective of the event.

Rapid cognition is a process that is present in everyone, and while it can, of course, be further harnessed and be put to more effective use, it is something in which the base "amount" is present nearly equally in all people. This is so because rapid cognition is our new fancy terminology for knee-jerk decision making. It's an evolutionary defense mechanism which is one of the reasons we are still an ongoing and thriving species. As a caveperson, if you saw a bear or something else that was without a doubt dead set on killing you, you don't have the time to understand and look in depth as to what may be causing this behavior in the bear. You have the time to understand that they bear is going to kill you if you don't react, so you react. However, I recognize this is perhaps a vague example of what rapid cognition is and how it can be applied to more a modern life, so let's look further.

Say you're on a double date with your partner or spouse, and a close friend of yours has joined you with their partner. This is the first time you've met their partner, but something doesn't feel quite right about that person. You can't quite put your finger on it, but something about them screams that they are not the person they might be making themselves out to be. You may feel that they might be a potentially dangerous person to you or your friend. At first, you don't tell your friend about your feelings—after all, you haven't talked to them much, it's probably just paranoia, right? Later, a few weeks or a few months down the road, you meet to catch up with your friend over lunch, and they mention that they're no longer seeing that person. Part of you feels relieved, but you ask why. Your friend sighs and admits that they caught their partner cheating on them a few nights ago. Part of you inside just jumps for joy, overjoyed that you were correct and excited about this newfound ability of yours. Or is it actually a newfound skill of yours after all?

The short answer is no. Although it would be a nice pleasantry to assure ourselves that we're actually magic or possess psychic abilities, here's what really happened—you saw your friend's partner and almost immediately knew something wasn't right. Whether it was by the way they carried themselves, the rather saccharine way they spoke to your friend, or the tone of their voice, something about them just left a kind of sour taste in your mouth. Whether you actively realized it or not, your brain—or at least, the subconscious part of it—picked up on some of these things without letting your conscious brain know. Your conscious brain was more focused on your food, on your partner, your friend, or otherwise preoccupied with a multitude of many different things. Your unconscious brain filtered through the massive amounts of information you picked up from this new individual. Your unconscious and conscious brain alike will automatically react more alertly to new individuals, if only because they are unrecognized and their speech patterns, body language, and habits aren't yet familiar enough to be discarded automatically. Your unconscious self understood and registered that a lot of the behavior displayed by this new person as habits that you would find unappealing or otherwise problematic. Your unconscious then gives that information back and stores it away, where you will feel unsatisfied or uncomfortable because of that person. Your unconscious won't register why because it never had the opportunity to process anything about the person because they never did anything overtly upsetting to you or to anyone else who was at the double date, so the conscious never really bothered with it. Your unconscious mind then proceeded to pick up the metaphorical slack where the conscious left off, processing more detail-oriented information that was more biased and therefore didn't particularly concern the conscious. Your unconscious mind acts more as a crutch which sifts through the information at hand and the stimulus that the conscious mind simply can't be bothered with sorting.

Now, before you go and run with every gut feeling you ever get and consider if fact just because you felt a hunch, remember to be cautious gut feelings. Remember that we discussed that unconscious decision making is partly based on past experience and bias, whereas the conscious is more prone to make decisions based on obvious fact. This is why the subconscious mainly deals with decisions based on someone's past actions and does not make a lot of judgements based on minimal interaction with new stimuli.

Although you may or may not have a large amount of trust in your unconscious decision making skills or a lot of faith in your gut, the decisions made by the unconscious are hunches. Rapid cognition is a collection of hunches. A lot of rapid fire estimates that were either immediately denied or inconclusive, help form a basis on which to understand that person based on those roughly educated guesses. If you meet people similar to you this may serve as proper evidence to condemn or to raise the status of that person to you and your conscious.

Please, don't follow your gut if you actually have facts and real experience with that person you could rely on instead for understanding a situation. Your gut and rapid cognition are brilliant tools that can be used in a major time constraint, but if you have the time and the energy, there may not be a direct need for it in every situation. We no longer live in an age where things like that are necessary, where a split-second decision is also the difference between life and death. Although making rapid cognitive decisions is an important part of honing your skills as a psychoanalyst, it's not necessarily a function that should be the first tool you grab. Although, admittedly it is a great tool that will serve you well when needed in your search for information in the world around you, and its most interesting inhabitants with whom you find yourself surrounded.

Chapter Ten: What It All Means

So, you've read—or, more likely, you've skimmed—through this information. We have covered persuasion and manipulation, misconceptions about personality tests, the rapid cognition and the masked legend from Japan. You've read and hopefully understood better what exactly it means to be able to psychoanalyze people. Hopefully, you now understand at least a little better what that actually means to you and for you, as a person. Hopefully, you understand what that means in terms of your personal growth, your interpersonal growth, and in the growth of your skills and abilities that will undoubtedly be underway for quite some time, likely until you leave the Earth.

But, what does it all mean to take all of the information we have given you over the course of this book and to sum it all up in a final summary? Let's look at a final analysis of what it means to psychoanalyze and how best to do it without betraying your moral code or invading people's privacy.

The beginning of our summary is, simply put: You do not have to have a degree or even really have more than a very basic understanding of human psychology to be able to analyze someone. Psychoanalysis is, in a sense, a kind of skill that is innately buried within many humans. Individuals who suffer from a neurodivergence may have difficulty with this basic built-in understanding of social cues and behavioral dynamics. Psychoanalysis is a big and complicated word that gets thrown around, but it is attainable. Put in its simplest forms, psychoanalysis is the ability by any given person to be able to look at a person for really any given period of time and be able to give a rough estimate on that person's personality, or at least be able to comment accurately of any aspects of the person. You may be able to see in a short period of time enough information that will help you quickly make decisions for a longer period of use.

We, as humans, connect in a very, very strange way sometimes. We have this odd way of connecting with one another in a hazy and often plain messy way, like puzzle pieces that really only form a coherent picture if you fiddle with the edges of the shape a little bit. We're all just sentient individuals unknowingly following trends and mirroring our friends as we seek a good life, however that good life may try to find us. No matter the scenario, we're all human. This philosophical sense of camaraderie goes beyond the late hours of the night in which we gaze wishfully upon the stars and contemplate why we're here. This sense of togetherness we get fuels our desire, our strange and often morbid compulsion to connect. Many may ask why we have this compulsion to meet new people and to do new things. Some people may deny their connection to the mass of the population entirely, insisting that they're somehow inconceivably different from the crowd. It does happen that when humans buck the course of tradition that we create a new in a way that, in its own right, becomes yet another trend for the general populous to follow.

We have a compulsion to interact and try and force ourselves to connect often simply for the selfish sake of knowing what we perceive to be the truth. If we feel that we know, we automatically hold a little bit of something above all of our friends, our peers, our enemies, and we want desperately to have this feeling of being separate, or even better in some manner. Sometimes people tire of this universe we find ourselves in and try to go forward in a way we've never truly seen in in the past. This is especially the case sometimes for people who live a manner where the main goal of life is to just get by and try to survive. Teenagers may feel that they just want to get out on their own as soon as possible. Families living in poverty or in financially restrained situations may feel as though they can barely survive and want to seek a new and better way of living. Some may not feel a financial strain but have other serious problems for which they must daily seek answers in order to survive. Some may adopt something similar to a social conflict theory, the sociological paradigm first proposed by famed communist Karl Marx, who proposed that any given society is little more than a boxing ring or colosseum for white collar and blue-collar workers to duke it out in an eternal and never ending fight to keep or take control from the other party. This way of looking at the world may seem morbid and pessimistic, but "if the shoe fits" as they say. There are, of course, several more optimistic or at least, more fair ways to look at the world around us. For example, structural functionalism dictates that every group and faction within society works like a well-oiled machine. Social interactionism, which hypothesizes that perhaps it is not the entirety of society which is interacting in a way causes it to produce itself, but instead that society as a whole is completely manifested in more obvious, simple, and innocuous ways so that at least two individuals will interact with each other at any time. This concept also notes that there are no true "raw" realities in the world, only well known "facts" that may only be viewed as factual to those who have at one point agreed to give that so-called "fact" validity. These paradigms all work together to in a way that divides sociologists and philosophers in their views on how society operates and can change. Such concepts will likely continue to be the source of much debate and much argument among highly regarded officials, even in today's modern era.

And in this modern era we live in now, what is there to be gained from the art of psychoanalysis? In a sense, haven't we already discovered everything there is to know about the human mind the psyche, and taught even taught much of it to our children?

No, of course not. Unlike many subjects like mathematics or physics, that may seem to have a more finite amount of information that could potentially be obtained, psychology is developing more and more every single day. From the physical aspects of psychology, we're discovering more about things like brain plasticity, which is the innate ability of the brain to shift its needs and operative parameters. We have learned that the brain is not actually a static or unchangeable organ, as we once thought. Studying the size and many functions of the brain's lobes and sections helps us to discover more about mental illness, disease, and concepts of behavioral psychology. We're rapidly learning more and more about all kinds of these mental illnesses and how best to treat and, better yet, prevent them.

Something else we learn more and more about every day is the psychology of ourselves. As psychoanalysts, the most important part of being able to analyze someone is being able to thoroughly analyze the person you undisputedly know the best—which is, of course, yourself. If you're not able to tell why you might do certain things or what your body language might indicate about your current emotional state, how could you ever hope to tell these things about someone else? It's like saying you could probably hit a fish moving through a stream with an arrow but neglecting to even practice on a stationary one on land. Overestimating your abilities is the downfall man in all professions—including psychological background. Some of the most pompous over-estimators of their own capabilities will be people who think that they have an undeniable iron grasp on the psychology of all humans because they believe that nihilism, which is a rejection of all moral principles, is the answer to everything.

This is the type of person may actively try to spread their own negative gospel, or perhaps they believe they are above optimistic people because they believe they suffer the burden of higher knowledge, as compared to fellow psychoanalysts and individuals analyzed.

This kind of person is also trademarked, so to speak, by their own consistent way of looking at people. Nihilistically minded people often perceive man as a predetermined malicious beast, and that humans are bound to be what they would call "evil," There are also some who would call humans inherently "good," perhaps due to their past experiences, to their faith or religion, or perhaps simply so that they feel they have appeased their own moral compass. In any case, most sociologists agree that both of these standpoints are wrong, when phrased curtly and in opposition to their own personal thinking. Most professionals who specialize in any kind of field that would pursue the reasoning of man may often agree that humans are not inherently "good" or "evil." They may choose professional behaviors that mean neutral concepts and actions must be employed in their collective interactions for the sake of those they seek to help.

We are all living in the same timeframe, on the same Earth, and some people are even reading this book within the same country. We may even be living in the same state or city. We are all coexisting, yet constantly battling at the same time. We are all interacting with one another, giving meaning to the world. Yet, in the very same instant that those micro-interactions are translating into massive interactions between white collar and blue-collar workers, between male and female, between ethnic groups and spiritual or religious factions, and between societies as bonded entities. So, in that sense, all three of the sociological paradigms we mentioned earlier are needed in their own respective format. We need a variety of viewpoints of the universe, so that we may understand it better and be able to view it from different points of understanding. If we allow ourselves to co-exist on opposing sides of a planetary body, we will be more likely to be able to view it properly as a whole planet. We can compile our information about that planet that are important to us to create a more colorful, descriptive, and developed view with greater accuracy if we do it together. Each person can still retain their own point of view, many of which doing the same thing, as they breathe the same air.

And yet, in this strange Schrodinger's cat-styled state of society that includes both calm and chaos, we find ourselves united through small and seemingly unimportant times in our lives. When we look upward toward the moon in the dead of night, we are often comforted by the knowledge that no matter how far away they may be, our loved ones are "beneath" the same moon. No matter where we travel or how far away we seem to feel from the people we love most, many of us believe we are all connected intrinsically through the firm ground we all walk upon daily. Remember this and be calm whenever you feel you may be swept away by the current of your daily life, and of the daily struggles that bind humans even more closely to one another. Seek the companionship of someone you can trust and enjoy watching their differences shine and fascinate you as you learn to appreciate your own personal uniqueness.

We are all bound together in that we have plenty to discover about ourselves as humans. What binds us so closely and so tightly together, is that we are all ignorant compared to what our collective knowledge as a species may be able to tell us if we were able to properly compile it. As Socrates once said in a famous work from Plato, "I know that I know nothing." Although it is perhaps intended as a simple paradox, a trick on the mind meant to confuse a reader, it may offer a much deeper insight into man itself. We feel we are aware because of our sentience, but how much further can we actually analyze our sentience? How can we prove to one another— and even to ourselves—that we are sentient? This is one of the many questions you may be left to ponder in your thoughts as you unlock the many psychological skills you have had locked away within you.

Part 2: Enneagram

An Essential Guide to Unlocking the 9 Personality Types to Increase Your Self-Awareness and Understand Other Personalities So You Can Build Better Relationships and Improve Communication

Chapter 1: History and Origin of the Enneagram

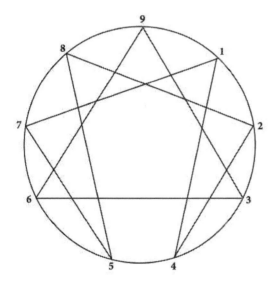

The history of the Enneagram of Personality is widely disputed, but there are some main points that are agreed upon as major contributing factors. There certainly seem to be roots that can be traced back to the philosophy of Ancient Greece. Some will emphasize the mathematical and geometrical qualities and evoke Pythagoras and Boethius; others point to its connections to the tradition of Kabbalah. These various traditions make up the framework that expresses the intrinsic archetypes that can be found in the Enneagram of Personality and serve as perspectives and traditions to consider when approaching the use of the Enneagram for self-development.

Platonic Essentialism serves as a founding for many of the archetypes and symbolic systematology involved in the foundations of the Enneagram. Basically, this comes from the philosophy of Aristotle and Plato, and it states that every person has an "essence." This "essentialism" is a core human concept that alludes to the Essence of the soul. The idea is firmly rooted in the belief in the existence of the human soul as a concept. Platonic essentialism was germinated in Greece and Asia Minor. Eventually, the ideas moved, as spices and materials did, geologically south, to areas now known as Syria and even further to Egypt. It was in these places that the ideas were adopted by early Christian mystics who focused on the ways that the divine form was lost in the ego. This is the origin of the Christian concept of the seven deadly sins. The original inspiration for the Christian seven deadly sins was contained by the same material that contained the nine types in the Enneagram.

Most scholars agree that it was the Sufis, people from the sect of Islam that emphasize mysticism and ecstasy, who developed the concept of personality types. They were spiritual and mystical people, who did a lot of work in the area of spiritual research. The Sufis' culture was deeply ingrained with mysticism. It was under their influence in the 14th and 15th centuries that the idea of personalities became defined. It was a Sufi belief that there were nine essential patterns or orientations to life. These patterns and orientations represented the image of God that exists within a person. There is also the other side of this representation: the opposite force within the person, which serves to block the realization of the power within.

The Sufis had a tradition of spiritual development that encouraged people to find their way to God over many years, and they witnessed from direct observation the nine ways in which individual personalities manifest and how they run into obstacles in their journey. To condense the Sufi's primary question, one could put it like this: What happens? What happens to our original goodness? What happens along the way to cause us to be distracted, or anxious, or too angry to have clarity in our lives? The Sufi's philosophy is congruent with Plato's. They had a conception of the human experience that agreed with essentialism, providing a means to reach self-actualization and self-realization.

The Sufis' believed that our psychological and spiritual development—our experiences, our upbringing, our attitudes, and positioning in the world—grow a tension between two dualistic truths that are available to each aspect of us: the virtue, or essential truth that mimics the divine form, or the vice, which serves to distort and subvert each virtue. You can see how this has directly influenced the Enneagram. Each Enneagram type has an essential vice and an essential virtue. These are traits that they naturally embody, and either might spring up in the face of challenges. Each type's virtue and vice can tell you a little about how they position themselves in the world and in their ideas.

Think about the way that our upbringing and context influence the way our personality is expressed. If a child grows up in a chaotic household, an environment in which she must protect herself, then she will develop ways to protect herself. The most developed and often used parts of the child's personality will be the ones that serve as protection. This could manifest itself in many ways, whether the strategies are good for the child or not. Once these behaviors and attitudes are firmly established, a person feels like they have an identity, and the ego starts to take hold. We then develop strategies to protect the undeveloped parts from criticism.

The Sufis had a beautiful, long tradition of meditation and prayer and mysticism. This path toward spiritual guidance has led the Sufis to integrate many concepts with spirituality. As their mathematical capabilities grew in the fifteenth century, Sufi mathematicians discovered the decimal system. This led to the concept of periodic decimal fractions (when one is divided by three or seven). As their scientific and mathematical understanding of the world grew, this knowledge was incorporated and fused into their spiritual understanding, and the Enneagram was one of the products of this marriage of science and faith. In the nine points of energy that the Enneagram describes, the Sufis saw nine refractions of the one divine love. The word Enneagram itself comes from the Greek words *ennea* ("nine") and *gramma* ("letter)".

The Sufis' understood the potential for insight in exploring our vices. The Sufi tradition asks, "What do our negative qualities teach us?" and it encourages the idea that positive and enriching value can be gleaned from exploring our negative sides. Before we can move on and understand ourselves, we have to look at how we are benefitting from the vices.

Kabbalah is a mystical ancient strain of Judaism. It is at once a school of thought, a method, and a discipline of Judaism. It contains the Tree of Life. The Tree of Life is a symbol in Kabbalah that is said to be a map illustrating various aspects of the world and our experience in it. The Tree of Life offers another interpretation of the divine forms which are manifested in our behaviors. The Kabbalah has nine Sefirot, which correlate with the Enneagram. Point One aligns with Hochma (all-knowing, correct, internalized father, Abba), Point Two with Bina (understanding, controlling, supernal mother), Point Three with Gedula (impetus, to be great), Point Four with Tiferet (beauty, romantic longing, point five with Din (bound, enclosed, limited), Point Six with nezeh (enduring, seeking authority), point seven with Hod (splendor), Point Eight with Yesod (seminal force), and point nine with Shekhinah (accepting presence).

Because of its wide-reaching, possibly universal roots, the Enneagram seems to be mostly congruent with most major religious traditions. The Enneagram is known in the Christian tradition to be a bridge between spirituality and psychology. With some research, we can see how the system of the Enneagram fits in with multiple secular and sacred sources regarding vices and virtue, or intelligence and weaknesses. Multiple ancient personality systems are contained in variants of the Enneagram model in Christianity, Sufism, and Judaism. This implies that the Enneagram has an ancient and common resonance with many peoples of the earth. In the table below, four ideological interpretations are made of the concepts contained in the Enneagram.

Enneagram	Kabbalah	Capital Sins	DSM-V
1.) The Perfectionist	Hochma—All-knowing, correct	Anger	Compulsive
2.) The Giver	Bina—Understanding, supernal mother	Pride	Histrionic
3.) The Performer	Gedula—Impetus to be great	Deceit (self)	Narcissist (secondary)
4.) The Romantic	Tiferet—Beauty, romantic longing	Envy	Depressive
5.) The Investigator	Din—Bound, enclosed	Avarice	Avoidant
6.) The Loyalist	Nezeh—Seeking authority	Fear	Paranoid
7.) The Enthusiast	Hod—splendor	Gluttony	Narcissist (primary)
8.) The Protector	Yesod—Seminal force	Lust	Sociopath
9.) The	Shekhinah—	Sloth	Obsessive-

Peacemaker	Accepting presence		compulsive

Ivonovich Gurdjieff has a significant place in the history of the Enneagram. He was a Russian adventurer and seeker who had studied Tibetan, Sufi, Indian, and Christian mysticism. Interestingly, Gurdjieff became aware of the Enneagram in Afghanistan. Gurdjieff didn't use the Enneagram as a typology of personality, however. He saw it as a sort of philosopher's stone, which had deep resonance in the archetypal experience of humanity. Gurdjieff's Enneagram seems to have come somewhat directly from the Kabbalistic Tree of Life. Gurdjieff's work laid the foundation for Oscar Ichaz0's work.

The most modern significant phase of the development of theory around the Enneagram was in the 1960s and 70s, during the work of philosopher Oscar Ichazo. Ichazo was native to South America, and after visiting various parts of Asia, he returned to Buenos Aires to develop his ideas, and eventually created the Arica School. The Arica School consisted of a system of psychology influenced by metaphysics and spirituality, based on the centuries of enrichment around the Enneagram symbol, created to help people reach new levels of self-realization. Ichazo's new conception of the Enneagram acknowledges the influence of mystical Judaism, Christianity, Islam, Buddhism, and ancient Greek Philosophy. He saw his work as a way to make clear the relationship between our essential selves and our ego-selves. To Ichazo, there is a potential in each human to be at harmony with the world, to be thriving against its challenges and settling in when there is comfort and ease.

The Enneagram is a topology; it is not unique in this, and there are various other systems of typology for personality. Astrology, for example, finds twelve categories for types. Psychologist Carl Jung, in his writings, uses the premise that there are three pairs of functions that are expressed differently in each person: extroversion-introversions, perception-intuition, and thinking-feeling. In each case, a person will favor one of each, leaving us with eight distinct personality types. Jung's archetypes also support and enrich the Enneagram. Jung's archetypes and how they relate to the types of the Enneagram will be discussed later.

The Briggs Myers typology is one that has been widely used since its conception. Isabel Briggs Myers developed this system by considering a different set of functions. Those are judging-perceiving, the inclination to quick, clear judgments and decisions as opposed to receptivity to many influences and kinds of information. She eventually developed the Myers-Briggs Type Indicator, a test that distinguishes among the sixteen personality types it includes.

The psychoanalyst Fritz Riemann was influenced by astrology when he worked out a scheme of human fears. He assumes four basic human fears: the fear of nearness, fear of distance, fear of change, and fear of permanence. This results in Riemann's four basic types: Schizoid, depressive, compulsive, and hysterical.

The guiding principle for all of these different models of personality classification is that all people are different, but some individuals have experiences and behaviors and attitudes that are remarkably similar to one another. A typology can be thought of as a sort of map that has the purpose of facilitating an overview of the soul. The Enneagram is a circle whose circumference is broken up by nine points. The points are numbered clockwise from 1 to 0. Points 3, 6, and 9 are bound together in a triangle, as are 1, 2, 4, 8, and 5, and 7 in a hexagon.

Chapter 2: The Types

The Enneagram of Personality describes nine contrasting worldviews and perspectives. These can be seen as strategies to navigate the journey of life. They can also be described as patterns. The theory of these personality types isn't that they describe a perfect individual or a bad individual. Rather, in each of the types is contained a pattern that develops in many ways and directions. For example, the Protector, or Type Seven, has the capacity to use their power and intensity for incredible good and the wellbeing of others, or for unspeakable evil. The listed characteristics that go with each type can be considered coping mechanisms, or habits, strategies; they can be developed in a skillful manner or an unskillful one. In the initial description of each type, there are some classifications. The Triad, which will be explored in more depth later, describes some of the basic drives and fears of the nine types that are divided into three groups. The Spiritual Focus of the type is where they find their general focus as an individual most of the time, for better or worse. The Strength is an example of one common adaptive characteristic of the type, and the Weakness is one example of a maladaptive characteristic of the type. The Positive Direction describes a positive path for growth that is commonly seen among the specified individuals. The Essence is about a person's positioning in the world, the authentic way they see beauty in the world. This brings us to the Secure Embodiment and the Stress Embodiment. Types tend to shift a little in personality to embody characteristics of other types when they are stressed, and similarly, people will also change their personality when they are feeling secure and positive. The Secure Embodiment shows which personality type a given type tends to shift to when they are at their best. The Stress Embodiment shows how a certain type tends to change when they are feeling worried, anxious, stressed, or otherwise unhealthy. The last category in the initial description types is the Wings of each personality type. For each type, they tend to act more like the types situated right next to them on the circle than the other types. For example, a Seven will act more like an Eight and a Six than any of the other types. They are closer in the way they perceive the world. Take a look at the descriptions for each of the types and consider how you and other people you know relate to them.

Type One Is the Perfectionist

•Triad: Defender

•Spiritual Focus: Correcting error, a right and wrong mindset

•Strength: Moral compass

•Weakness: Error

•Positive Direction: From criticality and judging to serenity

•Essence: Perfection

•Secure Embodiment: The Enthusiast

•Stress Embodiment: The Romantic

•Wings: The Peacemaker and the Giver

Personality Case Example 1

Deirdre is a business manager at a large local credit union. She oversees the majority of their operations and is responsible for a great deal of supervision. Deirdre is known as a meticulous woman, who plays it safe and pays attention to the details. She does her best when she can fill her life with organization and timeliness, and she likes things to be neat. It took her a few years after she started working in her current environment to get her office how she likes it. She likes design that is minimalist and simple. Deirdre really dislikes distracting noises and moved her private office to the other side of the building from the busy lobby. Her office is very peaceful; sounds are muffled, and it has a sense of privacy.

Neatness and order are a prerequisite to work with Deirdre. The top of her polished desk reflects the sun shining perfectly through the window, which has not a speck of detectable dust or smudging. The office plants are well kept and beautiful. Files are very delicately labeled, and everything is coded by color and format.

Deirdre is sometimes required to be a sort of salesperson; she despises this. Usually, she is able to push those duties off toward sometime else. However, even when she does, she provides strict supervision to make sure that every aspect of the business is running well. She writes extremely detailed memos. Everything needs to be very clear so that the message is understandable and will not be misinterpreted. Since she started as the business manager, the credit union's operations have been running more smoothly than ever before. What she has brought to the company is a sense of accountability and responsibility.

On Saturday nights, you can find Deirdre at the Howling Moon, a local pub and music venue, playing the fiddle at the bluegrass music open jam. She and other bluegrass musicians gather to pick and play songs, to share laughter, and to practice their skills. Almost nobody knows that Deirdre does this. She finds it a huge release to play her fiddle in the dim-lit hall, improvising and sometimes even singing until late at night.

Personality Case Example 2

Steven is the head supervisor at a contracting firm in Colorado. It is a rural area, and often the job includes traveling around their remote region of the state to take jobs. He is often on the road driving for hours. He doesn't mind this; however, he finds that he can still be productive on car rides. He sometimes will record instructions on his phone or spend the time on conference calls with clients or coworkers. Steven sometimes will listen to recordings of motivational talks or self-improvement programs in his truck on these long drives. Sometimes, he'll put on a Willie Nelson album, and get lost in thought but only sometimes.

Steven has a good sense of instinct on how to present himself. He wouldn't be able to answer how he has arrived at this, but he just knows what works and what doesn't. He can wear his Carhartt coveralls when meeting with ranchers out in the hills, but when he travels to Denver, he puts on his cowboy hat, nice shirt, and bolo tie. Steven is surprisingly judgmental sometimes of people who have not dressed appropriately for an occasion. He'll see someone and label him or her as a "bum" or "silly kid." Usually, he keeps his critiques to himself, but sometimes he becomes angry, and those who work with him know that his judgments can be harsh.

Once, a foreman had accused him of being callous, and Steven really felt the sting of this comment. It felt like a damaging truth that could be used against him. Sometimes, Steven has difficulty keeping workers around; they tend to lack a sense of trust in him. He doesn't trust his coworkers, but he has a need to make sure that everything is exactly right and often checks after people's work too much. He feels that he is responsible for every single detail.

Steven has noticed how much criticism affects him and tries to be gentle when he is criticizing others. It's just part of his nature to obsess over things.

Issues aside, Steven has an excellent reputation as a supervisor and has defended the company on countless occasions when things got tough. He also defends his workers from the sometimes-unrealistic demands of the higher-ranking managers at his company. He makes sure that the system he works for is fair.

The Type Ones are idealists, striving for truth, justice, fairness, honesty, and moral order. They are often very good leaders but have trouble accepting their imperfections and the imperfections of others, offering too much criticism of themselves and others.

The family of origin and the childhood experience are always integral parts of why a person is the way they are. The Perfectionist generally tried to be a model citizen from very early in life. In early childhood, the Perfectionists were told to be good, behave, try hard and work hard, don't be childish, do it better. Often, the parents of a Perfectionist will be moralistic or eternally dissatisfied. They may find difficulty in praising their children to the appropriate degree or take above-average goodness for granted. The Perfectionist learned to produce this "goodness" because they were afraid of losing the love of the parent. The Perfectionist will find themselves with the fear of losing attention and love and will meet the excessive expectations of his or her mother and/or father.

Type Ones try to be good so that they won't be punished. As the Perfectionist moves into adulthood, they will often find that they have internalized the voices of these demanding figures in their childhood. The voices may evoke thoughts of "self-sacrificing," goodness, or generous action. The ultimate question that these voices are often asking is, "Are you good enough?" Inside the Perfectionist, the court is always in session. The prosecution brings up examples of when the person was not good enough, or how they could never be good enough. The defendant, strong at first, offers up instances where the person did enough but never quite won the case.

Now, there's a bit of moralism, idealism, and perfectionism in almost everyone, but the Type One takes this instinct front and center when dealing with the world. Thus, the Perfectionist's key vice is the search for perfection. Sometimes, a Perfectionist will have a beautiful experience. One they are completely taken in by: a beautiful sunset, a perfect painting or piece of music, or a person. A Perfectionist will meet someone who appears to them to be perfect at first—in the Perfectionist's mind; they fill the requirements of a perfect person. As the relationship progresses, the Type One will eventually find the flaws of the person and become disappointed. A common tendency for Type One is for them to become unhappy because the world around them is not what they think it should be.

Anger is the root of the key vice in the Perfectionist. The Perfectionist is ashamed of their anger and their flaws, and avoidance kicks into play. Anger is something imperfect. This it puts most Type Ones in a place of a dilemma. They may feel anger because the world is not perfect, but they cannot express that anger because showing anger makes them believe they are not perfect.

In extreme cases, the Perfectionist may be living a double life. In public, they are spotless, moral, and blameless. But in somewhere in the person's life, the repressed darkness shows itself, whether it turns out to be behavior, thinking, or disorder in other ways.

The reverse of the search for perfection is cheerful tranquility. This can be a great way for Type Ones to battle their search for perfection. Cheerful tranquility could also be described in part by the Buddhist-sourced idea or loving-kindness, a part of the mindfulness tradition. When a Type One strives for loving kindness or cheerful tranquility, they are letting themselves slow down, soften up, and accept what things mean without wanting them to be different.

Type Two Is the Giver

•Triad: Attacher

•Spiritual Focus: Needs of Others

•Strength: True giving

- Weakness: Own needs

- Positive Direction: From pride to humility

- Essence: Freedom

- Secure Embodiment: The Romantic

- Stress Embodiment: The Protector

- Wings: The Perfectionist and the Performer

Personality Case Example 1

Charlie teaches eight-year-old students in the third grade. This is what he wanted to do from childhood. He can remember pretending to be a teacher while playing with friends, lining up the neighborhood children in rows while he stood and delivered the lecture from a toy blackboard, a present he had received from his parents. He found himself a caretaker even back then. He earned verbal approval from the kids' parents, who thought he was adorable, and also from teachers. As a young boy, Charlie would stay behind after school so that he could help a teacher carry books to the car. However, he was choosy; he didn't help all of the teachers, only the ones who he judged would keep up the relationship. He never helped the art teacher.

He was a model student in college. Charlie chose to participate in activities in college that would build his resume in the most efficient way but kept himself busy with volunteering work, secretary of the rugby club, and other extracurricular responsibilities. He was recognized and popular with his peers and teachers, and he kept his pride for being able to be a facilitator and giver secret.

Charlie always knew what type of environment he wanted to create in the classroom. Now, he had been teaching in classrooms for thirteen years. His current classroom was created to be comfortable and feel safe for the kids. There were art supplies, plush carpet, stimulating materials, instruments, computers, all provided to the students in an organized and safe world. He loves to be the gateway to higher education for children, recognizing their strengths and encouraging them to try new things.

While he is aware of the praises and compliments that he receives behind his back, Charlie does not admit this to himself or others. Charlie knows deep down that he is a human and cannot be the most indispensable teacher in the world, but he tries to imagine that it is possible. He takes on many extra duties and helps far above anyone else in the school. He might even feel competitive sometimes when a third party appears to be providing as much help and assistance as he does. He loves to see previous students when they come back to visit.

Personality Case Example 2

Dawn is 45. She's gregarious and affable and has been practicing as a psychologist for fifteen years. She's been a bulwark of security and helpfulness at her behavioral therapy center that she has worked at for the last ten years. Originally, she studied psychology because she had heard the term "helping profession," to refer to counselors and therapists. She knew early in life that she liked to help people. She was always the one who gave of herself. She took very good care of her friends and family.

Dawn held her job in extremely high regard. She found it worth celebrating that she was given the honor of an established position working with people in order to help them. She is rock steady in her reliability. Others have come and gone, but Dawn has stayed working at the behavioral health center for ten years without interruption. She has seen how different personalities work with the clients and is always the go-to when students or younger professionals have trouble with documentation or other written matters. Dawn has had the opportunity to be promoted to the director of the center more than once but has refused. She loves the opportunity to work directly with people rather than having the responsibilities of the first-in-command.

Dawn does appreciate, however, when people express their need for her. The amount of work that she does at the center does not go unnoticed, and many feel like they couldn't do what they do without Dawn. This is very motivational for Dawn, and she gets a sense of approval from others this way.

Her center provides a variety of services, and Dawn takes on clients from all walks of life. Sometimes, clients will have experienced cases of severe trauma or have drug or alcohol problems. Sometimes, people have minor depression or are just over-stressed. Dawn feels very present in the individual sessions, even more than the group work. She cares very deeply for other people. Her clients can see this, and it has helped many people to change. Dawn also volunteers at a local food bank and seems to have a natural ability to make people smile. She has a strength that pervades a room and makes everyone feel valued. She knows this is true but would never admit this to herself or others.

Type Twos, the Givers, often will seek out relationships and work that aligns with their need to help others and give to others. They may find themselves in professions of education, healthcare, or psychology. They stand by others when they have to endure suffering, pain, or conflict. This gives the Giver a sense that they have a place in the world and that someone else is with them to help them (or need them) when they need it. The Giver often has faults that may be more difficult to see than other types. They may find that they have an excessive need for validation. They may find that their childhood experience was one of emptiness or sadness. This can be an environment that was lacking in security or empathy. Oftentimes, the Giver experienced a family of origin in which the love was conditional. They needed to fulfill a role in order to have love. Sometimes when people grow up in these conditions, they find it hard to look back realistically on their situation and may find that they have a rose-colored glasses view of their childhood. Once they look closer, it may be recalled that early on they had a feeling of having to be a support for the emotional needs of other family members. They may have had a feeling that they had to make themselves useful in order to be noticed and loved. Unlike the Perfectionist, the Giver does not get hung up on being "good." They want to be nice and helpful. They sometimes are convinced that they are just that, and no more than that. A caricature of a mother of a Giver may say something like, "All that I've done for you, and now you do this!"

The Giver is continually holding his or her finger to the wind to determine its direction; they are often times too influenced by their environment. Whatever the people around them say they are, they are.

A child who is a Type Two will make a grand entrance into the room, announcing his or her presence. They will be rewarded for this with attention and love and respond with vibrancy. When the attention fades, however, the Type Two fades and becomes despondent and loses energy.

When the Giver enters adulthood, they need to adjust to the real needs and relationship that come. Oftentimes, when a Giver has not been able to adjust their orientation as an adult, they will find themselves being needy and possessive. They seem to be saying, "Let me help you," but really the message is closer to "need me." Obviously, this can lead the Giver to be manipulated; many can see that the Giver has a propensity to give and give and not want anything in return except neediness.

This problem is one of identity. The Giver will change continually in order to meet the needs of whomever is present. This leads the Giver to have multiple selves, which can lead to a problem of integration of self.

In their partnerships, Twos may be very possessive. They may end up with partners who are weak or dependent. A classic constellation is a partnership between a Giver and an addict. Codependence is usually in play here, as the Giver helps the addict, puts up with everything, forgives them, and gives multiple chances. This, of course, enables the addict to keep up with their addiction. They are capable of being sweet and pliant until the moment occurs when they become very afraid of losing their place in love.

When someone finds himself or herself embodying these aspects of the Giver, they should find a way to surrender themselves. This is the pride of a Giver. They wanted to be everyone's garbage disposal, but when it is their turn to give up parts of themselves that are vulnerable, they're not able to take the place of the dependent one. This involves a fear of rejection and sometimes the feeling that "nobody likes me anyway." The key vice for Type Twos is pride. We see Type Twos having a difficult time finding real self-knowledge. Instead they may eschew it for an easier self-analysis that shows how they are to be only for others and not themselves.

The Giver has a hard time taking risks. This can serve not only to protect the individual from harm but also prevents the person from achieving what they might be able to achieve. They see sharing personal thoughts and feelings as risky. A sense of rejection or disapproval is a real bitter taste for a Giver. It goes against their nature.

In order to be on a path of growth, the Giver will often need to learn to experience their emotions more intensely. They will have to give up being a helper for a little while and focus on themselves. If the Giver does this, they will find that they can direct some of their helping power inward. This is very freeing for the Giver to experience, and they might find joy in this practice. It will allow them to be better supported for others.

Type Three Is the Performer

• Triad: Attacher

• Spiritual Focus: Tasks

• Weakness: Failure

• Strength: Leadership on behalf of others

- Positive Direction: From self-deceit to honesty

- Essence: Hope

- Secure Embodiment: The Investigator

- Stress Embodiment: The Peacemaker

- Wings: The Giver and the Romantic

Personality Case Example 1

John is known in the culinary world around his town as an incredible chef. At the age of twenty-four, just out of a top culinary school, he was appointed sous chef at a famous upscale sushi restaurant in Los Angeles. John spent summers during his education cutting his teeth in the restaurant industry in California. He was a charismatic leader even then. He was easygoing and easy to relate to for others.

Immediately, as sous chef, John proved himself to be worthy of the position, going above and beyond the duties to which he was assigned, often putting in extra hours or implementing new details that the chef had not seen in the past. He gathered a loyal following in the community as a talented young chef.

Soon, John was hired to be a head chef at another prominent restaurant in Los Angeles, where he worked closely with another well-known chef who had more years of experience than John. John developed excellent interpersonal skills and grew a huge network of fellow professionals and peers.

John now excels in various work environments, where he consults for successful restaurant businesses around the country and the world, and always seems to be reaching higher and higher in his achievements.

Personality Case Example 2

Morty is known as a role model in his occupation. He is an incredible scholar, leader, and athlete. When he was in school, he achieved to the highest degree, consistently making it to every class, determined to be the best. His first job was as a math teacher in a small but well-known private middle school. In addition to a full course load, he helped teach the film class and coached the cross-country team. He was married with a couple kids at this time, and after a couple of years in the classroom, he took on ever-increasing responsibility in the administrative department, until his third year when he was appointed assistant principal. That year, he also started, workshopped, and executed a summer program for at-risk youth from the area based on the concept that if you teach skills like focus, commitment, and vocational skills, you will help students with self-esteem.

At age twenty-nine, he applied for a job as the assistant dean at a large private high school with a very good reputation. He beat out all of the competitors for the job. While he was in the process of interviewing for the job, he heard from students on their complaints with the administration. They thought that the principal and the other staff at the school did not hear their communication and didn't pay attention to them. He made this one of his top priorities. In his first few months, he made himself accessible to the students by always leaving his door open and engaging in casual conversation with students. His students developed relationships with him, as he encouraged them and pointed out opportunities for them.

Morty set up a new system of student government that pleased both his staff and the students at the school. He improved on older procedures and pioneered new representation for the students, inviting them to speak at every single superintendent's and principal's public meeting. One of his weaknesses is impatience. Rather than waiting for other people to get stuff done for him, Morty took more and more on himself. He eventually became burned-out. After that, Morty learned to pick people he could rely on for support. He eventually achieved an almost legendary reputation as the "coolest" administrator, and his fellow staff respected his work.

Later in his career, Morty moved on and was appointed the head of a prestigious school.

The Performer often has special talents and may have an easy time getting things done and being efficient. They have a sense for sizing up tasks and the dynamics of work groups. They often radiate ease and assurance. This inspires confidence from others. They identify themselves with the group or community in which they work, and they are talented at keeping a group cohesive. Networking is big for the Performer. They have charisma, which can win them great influence and success in work projects and other pursuits.

Type Threes will often have great difficulty in perceiving their own feelings. They are also holding their finger to the wind, like the Giver, but they don't as care as much as if they are liked or are good. Instead, they want to know if they are successful, or if it seems like they are winning.

Performers draw their energy form their successes. They are achievers, and careerists, and often seek status. The role of achieving protects The Three from being able to get to know themselves. They see things as winning and losing.

In childhood, Performers may have been super-achievers and heard many people say to them that you can do it! This, beneficially, sometimes becomes a self-fulfilling prophecy. Most Threes can be optimistic, youthful, intelligent dynamic, and productive.

Threes are cool, successful types; they walk through life seeing what they want and then go get it. And they do get it, by working hard. They go to great lengths to see that their plan is successful. They want it to look easy and offhand and don't show how much they are trying for these efforts.

Efficiency is a great value for the Performer.

They tend not to listen very well and have the bad habit of filtering out criticism, as they see it as just extra to whatever they are currently trying to do. They have several plates spinning all the time. They want to know why we are here, what we are doing, and how we are going to accomplish it. They might insist that someone is a bore, or they might want to take control of people who they don't find stimulating enough.

One strategy for a Performer to shift into a place of security and growth is to slow down. Simply take time to observe the self and breathe. A Three may find that when they slow down, the feelings that they have been pushing back will raise a little closer to the top. This will allow the Performer to relate to their experience better and to relate to others. The Performer may not admit it, but they feel overwhelmed a lot.

Type Four Is the Romantic

•Triad: Attacher

•Spiritual Focus: What's missing

•Weakness: Ordinariness

•Strength: Unique creativity, empathy

•Positive Direction: From self-deceit to honesty

•Essence: Universal belonging

•Secure Embodiment: The Perfectionist

•Stress Embodiment: The Giver

•Wings: The Performer and the Investigator

Personality Case Example 1

Hazel is an artist, a painter at heart, but she teaches mathematics. She grew up in a rural part of Nebraska, with a family that looked down upon excessive displays of emotion or any emotion at all. She found out how to control her feelings early on, but they built up, finding a way to get out in her passion for drawing and painting. Her esthetic achievements and successes were acceptable for her parents: it is alright for a woman to have interests. There was definitely no chance that they would support a full-time pursuit of art, however.

So, she studied mathematics, looking for an abstract way to pursue art while masking it in a scientific field.

As a young woman, Hazel's most meaningful moments were those of beauty and relation, when she experienced someone else receiving her expression kindly. She had a lot of concerns, kindness, and spirit to share. Sometimes, she even found that a connection with an animal fulfilled her need to share the beauty of the world.

Hazel lost her mother at the age of eighteen. She felt so much love for her mother. When she tried to tell her mother how much love she had as she was dying, her mother was finally able to accept her expression. She later named her daughter after her mother and would tell her as a young child how much she loved her mother.

Hazel taught mathematics in a public school with many classes including over thirty students. The classrooms were old and ill-equipped. Hazel had the chance to be hired at a smaller, more expensive college but felt that she would have more impact on students' lives at the school where she currently worked. She chose to live and work in one of the most underserved school districts. Sometimes, she would work with English-as-second-language students to help them be able to learn in her class. She loves the study of mathematics and was able to pass on this love and the subject matter in a kind and gentle way. Sometimes the students would act rude and disinterested. Her concern and authentic interest in mathematics, as well as their lives, helped to develop a good reputation for her at the school. Many students would return to visit Hazel, and she would be heartened to hear of their journeys.

Hazel thinks about her art sometimes and feels a bittersweet feeling of melancholy. Sometimes she asks, "What if I pursued art fully?" When Hazel turned 45, she rented a small studio space in her town and began to paint again.

Personality Case Example 2

Roger teaches drama in the music program of a prestigious small-town liberal arts college. Growing up, Roger always knew that he loved theater and spent many years chasing a full-time acting career. He graduated from a great acting program and landed a few parts in off-Broadway shows. After college, he got a big break. Roger was cast in a show that had a tremendous amount of media buzz around it, and he knew that this was the production that could have launched him to the next level of his craft. However, Roger quit the production a couple weeks before opening night. Everyone said that he was crazy. This had been a huge opportunity, and he had been working on it for so long. "It was self-sabotage," they said. Roger just shrugged off their concerns. He said that he knew it was coming, because in life, the glass was always half empty. Roger had been told by his acting teachers in high school that he could do anything that he set his mind to accomplish. He was talented enough to rise to the highest level of professionalism. Roger realized how significant this early teacher was, and the connection that they had had kept him motivated for many years. He wanted to be like his teacher, to have meaning in his life. Roger decided to go back to school and become a drama teacher.

He became a very sought-after instructor. Sometimes, his passion was so intense that he provoked controversy. He had a unique love of literature and a respect for the level of skill that it required to create. He also was good at working with the performing arts students. It seemed that you hadn't had a real university acting student's experience unless you had taken one of Roger's classes. A student would come in and experience the rigor, the depth, and the demanding nature of his classes, and be hooked. He had a high-quality connection with his students.

The program grew under Roger's influence and came to have a significant reputation as a leading acting school in the nation. Now, Roger has taught there for about eighteen years, and he is a legend among the students. Older students will introduce freshman to his classes, their recommendation ringing true as the new student becomes enamored with Roger's teaching style. He always wears black pants, a black shirt, and some kind of creatively colored scarf. He has bright blond hair that he keeps long and looks like his own version of a rock star. His celebrity on campus grew and grew as he took some minor roles in independent films over the years.

The Romantic is driven by the need to be special. They put their talents to work to awaken themselves and others to the beauty that is around them in their world. They often express their feelings in art, dance, music, acting, or literature. They are deeply attracted to things that have vital energy. They grasp the moods and feelings of other people and the atmosphere of places and events with precision. They are spiritual people, and they understand the connector of the sacred and profane. They love the realm of the unconscious, of symbols and dreams and may prefer this world to the real world. Symbols help them to make sense of the world and to express themselves. They have a gift of helping others to develop an appreciation for beauty and art. They also draw their energy from others. They are asking the question to the world, "Say, do you notice me? Do I catch your eye?" They strive for esthetic accomplishment, to be exceptional, creative, esoteric, eccentric, or exotic.

The drawback to the spontaneity and creativity of a Romantic is that they may become artificial, in a certain sense. This can sometimes be similar to the Performer, in that they want other people to view them as nice and neat and perfect, in this case perfectly imperfect. They believe that the world will be saved by beauty.

In childhood, the Romantic often had the experience of meaninglessness and unbearable emotionality. Sometimes its related to the experience of a loss. This can be a real material loss such an as a grave catastrophe, or it could have been felt emotionally. Positive role models may have been missing in this person's upbringing. The child. in a search for identity, turns toward the inner world because cither the original source for love end affection was missing or was too worn.

The Romantic will sometimes find that they are directing anger related to a loss toward themselves. They believe that they are guilty and "bad." Shame is a common vice for the Romantic. They will find themselves over and over again stuck in situations which are not good for them. They will cultivate their "badness" in this way and, therefore, may keep perpetuating the behavior.

The Romantic tends to not think much of the norms of society, for the boring, everyday rules of society. They feel themselves to be strangers or outsiders. This gives them an elitist consciousness, which helps them to be mindful of justice.

A Romantic will sometimes fall into the trap of thinking that their inner longing will eventually result in some ultimate object of their desire being conquered, resulting in them being finally happy. They learn along the way that as soon as they possess an object of their desire (whether it be a relationship, job, or material goods), they will immediately be dissatisfied, as their longing becomes centered around a new ideal good.

The Romantic may revere great figures like important writers, musicians, or gurus, who have something deep within them to express to the world. They dislike things that are bland, stale, or average. However, they may be simultaneously romanticizing the lives of others and may have idealized versions of matters that they are not a part of in daily life. This is a tendency of which Romantics should be aware. It can lead to disconnection, an ivory tower-style attitude, and a distance from authenticity.

The key vice for the Romantic is envy. They see people around them with more talent, status, capabilities, or eccentricities than they do, and they can't accept their own place in the world. They may find themselves wondering how other people can be happy. They avoid ordinary things. Things that are conventional and normal evoke disgust.

Depression can see itself manifested at a significant rate with the Romantic, as they live in a sweet melancholy sadness that can take over their life. The Romantic who finds themselves trapped in their own sweet sadness can find that it becomes a fog that pervades life in a very disruptive way. For Romantics, death is something that they consider at length.

Fours need friends and partners who will bear with them without letting themselves be drawn into the mood shifts. They take their feelings very seriously and are offended when they are hurt.

For a Type Four, the shift into a growth of energy and security will involve feelings of a new sense of a moral compass, a new reality outside of themselves. This may manifest in new relationships, moving out of town, or finding another way to have a shift of perspective. The Romantic does this to clear the mind and find new meaning in a particular situation.

Type Five Is the Investigator

- Triad: Detacher

- Spiritual Focus: Gaining Knowledge

- Weakness: Connection

- Strength: Rationality

- Positive Direction: From hoarding to allowing

- Essence: Awareness

- Secure Embodiment: The Protector

- Stress Embodiment: The Enthusiast

- Wings: The Loyalist and the Romantic

Personality Case Example 1

James is a retail store manager. He has a problem of connection. He can be a very effective manager when he is in his element. He feels passionate about his responsibilities in the store. He feels great in bringing his work environment into a place of positivity, efficiency, and productivity. However, his subordinates often report that he is not passionate or responsive in the job and that there is a lack of interaction. James does not see this at first; he keeps his feelings and thoughts tucked away in secret. He always tried to keep an air of objectivity, to the point where people never knew his real feelings. He didn't want to show enthusiasm for one idea, at the risk of making other employees think that they didn't deserve praise. In the past, he was too careful to not criticize misguided ideas.

James places high importance on nonattachment. He tries not to let feelings interfere with his judgment. So, when employees come into his office crying, why is it difficult for him to be patient and supportive? James doesn't think that a verbal report is as reliable as written thoughts, and he has a problem providing helpful feedback, like a casual, "Nice job." He never becomes visibly happy about his business' success.

James sometimes speaks in a monotone when addressing his employees and likes leaving long silences when employees can't come up with explanations. He would rather connect with people by finding solutions together.

Eventually, with some introspection and counseling, James starts to be able to be himself a little more around his employees. James learns to not be so sarcastic and detached and starts to feel less like a fish out of water. He starts to express his excitement for the workplace and starts to make connections with employees. One employee even excels in the job to the extent that they are promoted and leave for a higher position.

James has a passionate side, and he loves to spend time hunting in the mountains on the weekend. This brings him peace and calm as he is methodically doing work that he enjoys, work that involves a lot of observing and investigating.

Personality Case Example 2

Father Robert is the directing priest for his diocese in Ohio. The cathedral at which he works is seventy-five years old, and it is known as one of the oldest structures of its kind in the Midwest. He heads the organization that is responsible for 100 clergymen. They range in age from a few new priests in their twenties to a lot in their fifties and older. Robert is nearing the age of retirement himself and spent only a few years preaching early in his career before he was chosen for larger duties at the diocese after five years on the job. He has a distinct ability to work with people as a preacher and also an administrator. He makes detailed memos and keeps a macro-vision of the needs of the church, and he has a great leadership style that makes him an asset to his diocese.

He is a tall man, and his aura matches his physical presence. When Robert walks into a room, people notice. He is a historian in some ways; he has researched many methodologies and lines of inquiry in regard to biblical interpretations and as a counselor to the people. He is an avid seeker of truth and meaning. He has a deep sense of humble quietness to his spirituality. He is beloved by the congregation.

In fact, Father Robert knows the names of most of the congregation members. He always tries to meet new church members and keep up his relationship with older members of the congregation. He likes to talk with people, eat with others in the church community center, and help teach Sunday school classes. He says that the innocence and spontaneity of the children rejuvenate the energy of the church.

Robert has to work hard to develop interpersonal skills that allow him to handle difficult and pressing issues with anxious parents or a stressed out member of his church. He is independently minded, and he stays aware of the drain on the energy that it takes to practice the diplomacy that he employs in his organizations. Sometimes, when he overworked, he finds himself becoming detached from the situations. He sees himself just going through the motions. If he could, Robert would prefer to just communicate through written notes and email. He likes to protect his time and believes that time is of the essence. Minimal emotionality translates into rational thinking, Robert believes. He thinks that his greatest achievement is being rational in his thinking.

Father Robert was one of the first priest leaders in the nation to see the potential for technology to change the way that the administrative duties of the church work. He was the first to buy an early Mac computer, and later, had Wi-Fi in the church before most businesses did. He runs a newsletter for the congregation. He has people from the community write articles and include news about the church. He likes the feeling of being on the cutting edge of technology. He thinks that you have to have an open mind to deal with the chaos of the world.

The investigator is driven by the need to perceive. They are careful people. They think before they act, and they act according to objective information. They can be quite open and vulnerable and receptive to new information. They are researchers, inventors, journalists, and explorers. They can be very original and provocative and tend to surprise people. They are good listeners, active listeners who pay attention. They help others to become more perceptive.

In childhood, the Investigator often experienced extremes in the unbalance of intimacy. It can be augmented by an experience of too much intimacy, i.e. a cramped, non-private living situation, or by a lack of intimacy, where the child received little tenderness and affection. When this happens, children lose the capacity to develop the skills to show their feelings or express them psychically. They sense an emptiness in themselves. It is caused by a lack of security and the feeling of being unmoored.

The Investigator has some qualities that are somewhat opposite to the Giver. The investigator is a taker. Always opposed to the Giver, the Investigator is obsessed with taking. They have a passion for collecting, which can manifest itself in thoughts, or the physical practice of collecting or even hoarding.

The Investigator is obsessed with concentrating on seeing everything, absorbing it like a sponge, they tend to be ascetics and internal librarians. They may be photographers or scientists, trying to take in all the world around them and make sense of it. They don't like feelings and ban subjective talk and fuss. They enjoy the precision, being able to maintain calm, at least externally, and keep their feelings sublimated. They often experience difficulties in relationships with people close to them. They are good at cherishing the abstract idea of a person, thinking of them in their faraway, abstract version but can't deal with the messy truths of actually being with people.

The Investigator should be wary of the tendency to be afraid of intimacy as they may avoid anything with passion and feelings. They generally want to be outside of the messy circle of human relationships. They might find themselves as the mystic monk living in a cave or in a shack out in the woods. They want to avoid attention and be the neutral intake monitor of information. They may have difficulty understanding that life does not always work that way. They could think of nothing more beautiful than to sit and look at something, or nothing at all.

There is the downfall here, of course, of being completely overpowered by what you've convinced yourself is "logic." They have what they believe as an understanding of the world. What they don't understand, they don't mess with for simplicity. The key vice here is knowledge. For these types, knowledge is power. The Investigator has a belief that they can be safe by having information and details about the world around them. Being informed by the world is never sufficient, as one finds that they must participate in the world, to really live in it.

They might use withdrawal as a defense mechanism. They are afraid of nothing so much as emotional engagement.

We can see here that the deep unresolved problem is the love of self. They fear that if they are vulnerable to the world, they will be destroyed. Perhaps they were taught this in their upbringing. This lesson to never be vulnerable can be a powerful, but maladaptive coping mechanism to deal with problems. They want to avoid emptiness.

The Investigator will have to learn to feel somewhat secure if they are to embody a secure self. They might experience the energy for this as a physical manifestation, as Fives are very visceral and can trust their gut instinct. They often feel rushes of energy. If the Five can learn to trust and learn from their physical instincts, they will find themselves better adapted to deal with challenges.

Type Six Is the Loyalist

•Triad: Detacher

•Spiritual Focus: Scanning to seek certainty

•Weakness: Deviance, being seen as different

•Strength: Sound cognitive logic, clear thinking

•Positive Direction: From self-deceit to honesty

•Essence: Faith

•Secure Embodiment: The Peacemaker

•Stress Embodiment: The Performer

•Wings: The Enthusiast and the Investigator

Personality Case Example 1

Tina works at a well-respected law office. She has a side-consulting practice, but her main job is as a public defender. She has written about law and has been published in law journals. Tina loves taking on a new case, standing in front of the crowd in a courtroom and presenting the case. This was not always what she enjoyed. In her first case during her first year of working as a lawyer, she was faced with a room full of her peers, and she was so afraid of the situation that she nearly gave up and quit.

She later found herself having a pep talk with herself. She told herself, you invested way too much time, energy, and work in this career to give up. It's too late to change your mind, and this is what you want. She spends the night reviewing her notes, checking for any vulnerability. Once she completed her review processes, she convinced herself that the argument was as strong as it could be. Nothing could go wrong. The next day, she woke up, performed well at the trial, and the next day, she woke up and did it again. Slowly, she became more able to get up in front of the courtroom with ease, but she never forgot that initial feeling of panic that she felt on that first day.

Over the years, Tina's lectures became well-known for their theoretical rigor. She inspired the staff of the courtroom to think with equal rigor. This was her goal of being a lawyer: to teach people, to be rock solid for her clients.

In her late forties now, she has been in law her position for decades and has been offered various administrative duties but has stayed in the gritty arena of the public defender. She is loyal to the practice and despite her desire to move up the chain, she likes her responsibilities as they are. She is a cautious woman, and she engages gently with others who want to rush through the task with ill-conceived plans or positions. This has made her an extremely valued lawyer. She begins to take on more and more important and influential cases.

Tina winds down her career as she grows into her fifties. She takes on fewer jobs and starts to be a more supportive person with law students who come to learn. She creates safe spaces for them as they pursue the field that she has excelled in herself.

Tina knows that she is a successful professional, but she also feels that at any moment, the universe could pull out the floor from under her and that when crises happen, she will feel that old familiar panic. She relies on the energy rush that she gets in intense situations, so she knows that she can cope with each crisis.

Personality Case Example 2

Patrick is a mesmerizing singer. There is no song that he cannot express with his powerful voice. He doesn't mess around with stage antics or ice-breaking. He just gets on the stage and sings. He doesn't move around a lot when he's on stage, and soon, the audience is drawn into his imaginative style that becomes as real as the bodies around them. His tone and dexterity and expressiveness build into the experience of a truly enlightened musician.

Patrick often has a sarcastic and caustic sense of humor and knows how to employ it to the benefit of the situation. He spent years studying the human voice and submerged himself in the exercises, health practices, and work that music requires. He has spent time studying music theory, world music, music history, and instrument theory. He also works as a vocal coach.

However, Patrick is at his best when he is on a stage with a microphone. It provides him with the artistic license to share his experiences with the world. Away from the protection of the stage, he might be known to people as crabby and paranoid. He has faith in music and for performing.

He lives in what would be called a somewhat sheltered existence. His apartment is a large loft-style abode near the music district of the city in which he lives. This is where he does all of his communications via phone and email booking gigs, contacting musicians, and practicing. He has a large extended family, and they know him as loving, caring, and funny. He has a few friends but not really close ones. He thinks that people are always trying to take advantage of him.

Patrick is driven by energy to push himself toward what interests him, talking through whatever problems come his way. There are a lot of problems there in the world, so he stays pretty busy. The energy that he gets from this lets him keep his career up, earn enough money to stay afloat and keep moving all the time.

These types are driven by the need for security and certainty. They are very cooperative. They are reliable team players. In relationships, one can always count on their fidelity. Their platonic relationships are often marked by warm-hearted and deep feelings. They are often highly original and witty; sometimes they have a grotesque sense of humor. The Loyalist who has adjusted well to their role in adulthood knows how to participate in important traditions with the readiness to take on new paths. They know what is possible and what isn't. They can help you find the weak points in your project.

Some say that the Loyalist is one of the most frequently encountered personality types.

The key vice for Type Sixes is fear and deceit.

They succumb easily to self-doubt. This makes them cautious, and if overtaken by this, they become fearful and have a hard time trusting people. They sense danger in almost every situation. In their worst form, they become victims to their own paranoia.

In childhood, you may find that a Loyalist was exposed to many anxieties and dangers and saw them as such. There is a sense of primal trust that must be developed in early childhood. Some Loyalists report that they could never get to that place with their parents because they were unpredictable, or violent, or cold. As a coping mechanism, these children either look for a protector who they can trust, or they learn to detect the slightest signs of approaching danger so that they could keep themselves anticipate what was going to happen.

In adulthood without adjustment, this may turn into the attitude that the world is dangerous, and you always have to be looking over your shoulder. They may feel that they cannot keep themselves safe and that they need others to keep them safe.

They are emotionally dependent on others and don't reveal a lot about themselves.

The Loyalist might find an unhealthy tendency to want everything to be black and white. They don't want to deal with gray shadows and impenetrable fog. Sometimes, they may be predisposed to political fervor, thinking that if they align themselves ideologically with one tradition, they will find security in it.

The Loyalist will face great obstacles to becoming a whole and independent person. At junctures of change in life, such as starting a new job, moving away from home, or other major changes, they might find themselves paralyzed. They may scrutinize every detail and eliminate all contradictions to their own way, losing the important perspective that family and friends provide.

They are pessimists and anxious about their own success. Being independent and successful will scare a loyalist. The Loyalist may easily view themselves a "loser." They participate in self-fulfilling prophecies about their failure in all realms of life. They have a hard time accepting praise.

The downfall of the Loyalist is their continual striving for security. The defense mechanism for Sixes is projection. They often have an imagination for scenarios of apocalyptic terror and often anticipate the worst-case scenario.

In order to manifest a higher stage for themselves, The Six needs to be vulnerable. They must put down the fear of everyone and everything, relax, and understand the unconditional love of another. A Type Six may find that they have deep insecurity. Whatever it takes to address these insecurities, find it for yourself. It may come from exploring past issues, or it may come from creating art or journaling. The Loyalists will need to be kind to themselves when going through this process.

Type Seven Is the Enthusiast

•Triad: Detacher

•Spiritual Focus: Plans and options

•Weakness: Pain

•Strength: Optimism

•Positive Direction: From no limits to restraint

•Essence: Commitment to work

•Secure Embodiment: The Investigator

•Stress Embodiment: The Peacemaker

•Wings: The Protector and the Loyalist

Personality Case Example 1

Karla is a national park ranger at Olympic National Park. She chose to be a park ranger because it allowed her the opportunity to frequently explore nature and be free in the wild. She likes young people, and she takes on lectures for students who visit the park. This gives her a sense of fulfillment and fun. Karla knows how to keep her work enjoyable. She travels to conferences for forestry workers and keeps abreast of the new perspectives in her field. On the side, she maintains a business growing vegetables to sell at farmers' markets.

Karla's passion is for travel, and she gets to travel a lot for her work. She views the world as her oyster to be traversed on a whim. Once, she had a love affair with a young man in the forestry industry in Arizona. She surprised him by treating him to a three-day weekend in Las Vegas. They danced, ate and drank, and seemed extremely compatible at the time. However, Karla soon broke off their relationship at the height of its promise. She felt too young and as though she couldn't settle down. Besides, she felt that she might meet many other attractive and compatible people in her life.

Karla has charm and an easygoing way with people, but with young people in particular. Students and coworkers alike appreciate her optimism. She has a sense of irreverence rooted in the belief of equality and can be blunt around people with power or those with less power than her.

Eventually, Karla was offered a higher administrative job at Grand Canyon National Park. She jumped at the opportunity to live in a new place and meet new challenges. She started fantasizing about her life in Arizona much before she actually moved there. Her colleagues and students were surprised to see such a quick change in her life. Karla just took it as the way she was meant to go in her journey of life. She isn't afraid of not having a job. She can't see the sense in setting limits for herself. She has faith that her future will turn out nicely.

Personality Case Example 2

Lucius is in his late thirties. He consults for a business firm and has had a varying history in different industries. In college, he was very interested in the creative fields, especially connected with literature, and he studied creative writing. He had a rock band, which became somewhat successful and allowed him to tour the country. The group had some money trouble in Colorado, so Lucius worked his way back to New York by taking various jobs, including an office job in an agricultural company, a rodeo clown, and a waiter in a large city. Lucius is interested in the pathways that connect to make up his life's journey. He has a curiosity about people and a sense of adventure. The life of freedom and on the road, these notions really spoke to Lucius.

He achieved his undergraduate degree and went on to study Semiotics in graduate school. He chose to work in Semiotics because, as he says, he has loved to be spontaneously intellectual, to be free in his academic pursuits, to let his mind fly into a fantasy world that he could create to appreciate art and literature. His first job as a consultant did not go so well. He was angry to learn of the limitations of the business world and felt like he wasn't experiencing personal growth due to being curtailed by the institutional regulations. He did not see himself as an authority figure.

The concept of a magic circle intrigued Lucius for a decade. After he eventually quit his consulting job, he went to the Pyramids of Egypt to experience the immense power of the ancient structures. This started him on a path of travel and study that eventually grew into a performing arts program based on the history and anthropology of the world.

Lucius was able to find foundations to support his work financially, and he now runs a non-profit that involves kids in cultural exploration through the history of art. He is sometimes hired by organizations around the U.S. that focus on integrating cultural experiences in schools and has spearheaded many new programs to increase arts in education.

Type Sevens are driven by the need to avoid pain. They are radiant, optimistic, and very alive. They are very mindful people. They can feel childlike in moments when others have difficulty. They have an immediacy to their spirit. They are full of idealism and plans for the future; they can pass on their enthusiasm to others. They are cheerful and love to be with people and children.

In childhood, the Enthusiast may have experienced an event that they felt was too much to hold inside themselves, and to avoid the repetition of the similar event in the future, they may evolve to repress their original negative experience. Many Enthusiasts paint their story in a positive light, suggesting that you can't let it get you down.

Have you heard that song "Tracks of My Tears"? That's about an Enthusiast. Smokey Robinson sings, "Take a good look at my face. You'll see my smile looks out of place. Yeah, look a little bit closer and it's easy to trace the tracks of my tears." It is the Enthusiast that has this permanent smile. The Enthusiast is the "eternal child." They are curious and need change, stimulation, and new environments and experiences. They have a calendar full of beautiful and exciting obligations.

The Enthusiast may find that procrastination and avoidance cause them trouble in life. Unpleasant tasks are thrust aside, put off, or ignored.

The key vice for Sevens is idealism, of a certain kind. They must be sure that they are working for a good cause. One result of this is that they deny and repress aspects of their activity that could have the slightest chance of hurting other people. This obviously leads to clashes between their needs and the needs of other people.

The Enthusiast who has shifted into a growth pattern will find that they relish privacy. Their mind doesn't slow down, and they like to be free to do their mental gymnastics on their own. A well-adjusted Enthusiast, however, will be able to balance the need for this personal leisure with other parts of life.

Type Eight Is the Protector

•Triad: Defender

•Spiritual Focus: Power and control

•Weakness: Vulnerability

•Strength: Empowering others

•Positive Direction: From excess to trusting sufficiency

•Essence: Truth

•Secure Embodiment: The Giver

•Stress Embodiment: The Investigator

•Wings: The Enthusiast and the Peacemaker

Personality Case Example 1

Martin found himself in an unbearable situation. He wanted to find a place where he could be an educator, but he simply could not put up with the public school system. There was just too much regulation, all to protect the power of the authority, and it was hard to get past these and get to the task of learning. He hated the small-mindedness that he found in the public school system.

However, his students in his middle-school classroom saw quite a different side of Martin. He had great ability and passion for helping them learn. This was his element, his territory, and he made the rules. Martin believes that education is about giving empowerment to young people. Truth and fairness are a big deal in Martin's classroom. Each year, the students would come in, and Martin would instruct them to put into words their commitment to keeping the class a safe place for everyone, to abide by the rules, do homework on time, and support the classroom environment. Martin had a policy of how to deal with situations in which a student was not honoring this commitment. His policy was thus: when a student broke the roles, he or she had to tell the class what if felt like to mess up. The other students told the student who had broken the rules how it felt to be in the room with them breaking the rules. Martin saw this as a way to engender justice in the kids. The issues of morality in the classroom were often black and white. He put people on the spot to help them to speak for themselves. The lesson that he wanted to impart was the value of truth. He believed that truth was the way to empowerment. Martin's classroom did provide challenges to the students. Some of them had a hard time dealing with the stringent nature of his classroom. However, Martin's supervisors supported him. Martin continued to try to take on the school system, but he eventually saw himself being outpaced by the regulations and bureaucracy of the school system.

Suddenly, about one year later, Martin resigned. He felt sad about abandoning the current cohort of students, but he rationalized that they would have an effective teacher with or without him.

After he had resigned, Martin became aware of a private school in town. He became interested in working there, thinking that he might find a better environment for his personality. One day, he marched into the office of the school president and asked if he could head the special education department. He got the job and learned to love helping the underdogs in the system. This proved a great feat of accomplishment for Martin, and he felt much more at home and free in his new position.

Personality Case Example 2

Alyssa is an attractive woman, lean, of medium height, and she has a tremendous presence. You can feel her assertive, almost belligerent energy preceding her as she approaches. She has been working as an auto mechanic for almost twenty years, though you'd never know it by looking at her. She had taken a couple of breaks, working various jobs, but always came back to the same old garage. When asked why she came back, she barks out her answer: "I like this place. I like the neighborhood. I like cars."

Alyssa always wears the same overall outfit, and she is a passionate worker. She has an intellectual power to diagnose and find solutions to mechanical problems. She leads her team of mechanics forward in a battle to victory over the body of work that they have to conger. Her vocabulary takes on a sort of militaristic bent. She plans a campaign, wages war, and doesn't take prisoners when there are only a few hours left in the day.

Alyssa is tough and finds herself often berating the younger generation, which she labels the "screen generation." She finds that they are always looking at a screen, letting life pass by them. She leads a battle in her own life against this, not allowing her kids to access screens before the age of ten. She is open when she finds someone being disrespectful by looking at their phone too much in public situations.

Some people love Alyssa but some people, not so much. She brings her intellectual energy into every environment that she finds herself.

Younger mechanics are extremely impressed by her skills, but at the same time are scared of her prowess and intensity. She has a lot of strong opinions. She will push and challenge a young mechanic, making them work harder than they thought they could, as she can see that they will be better mechanics than they themselves can see.

The Eight will impress you as strong and mighty. They have a sense of strength to their spirit and are able to care for and protect others. They instinctively know that there is something that "stinks" when injustice or dishonesty is at work. They can be a rock of stability, and they sometimes take on incredible amounts of responsibility.

The Eight is an interesting inversion of the One Personality. Instead of internalizing the message that they should always strive to "be good," they internalize the message that they need to be "bad," so that the world will function as it should.

Weakness and similar tendencies will only lead to suffering. The childhood of a Protector will often be characterized by repression and having been pushed around by others. They may not trust anybody but themselves.

They have the idea that you can't show weakness or cry. Some Eights reported that their parents rewarded strength over other values. They have the voice of, "Don't take it! Hit back! Show them who's boss!" This is the rule that the Protector abides by: don't back down, and don't show weakness. They sometimes are confused for the Perfectionist, but unlike the perfectionist, they are not easily able to admit fault. They developed the strength to resist, to break the rules, and to order others around rather than be a follower themselves.

One positive aspect of this is that the Protector rarely puts up with false authorities or unjust hierarchies. They have a passion for justice and truth. This often leads them to help and side with oppressed people. This is because they know that within their own deepest self, there is an inner child, which is the opposite of the strength that they project to the world. When the Protector is in power, however, their subordinates often feel oppressed, because the Protector is mostly oriented to protecting themselves.

Different personalities have different ways of making and sustaining human contact. For the Perfectionist, it may be involving people in a project that they are helping to make "perfect." For the Protector, a way of making human contact is actually fighting. It could be called confrontational intimacy. They enjoy struggles and conflict. They don't always understand that not all people feel the same about struggle and conflict. They don't notice how aggressive they can be. Conflict is their currency. Jokes may go awry.

They are often competitive and very good at games and sports. They have the ability to sense weaknesses of others, and they are good at taking advantage of the weaknesses of others.

The Protector often has the power to help others to reach their potential. This is how the Protector is able to harness the virtues that they are gifted with and to control the key vice, which is shamelessness. The protector's actual energy is not anger or rage, while sometimes it can seem that way. It is a passion and total commitment to truth, life, and justice; it is a passion for a cause they believe is important.

Don't let yourself be intimidated by Type Eights. They may make noise, but their bark is worse than their bite. They are often described as "larger than life."

The pitfall of the Eight is when they get obsessed with revenge and retaliation. They become the self-appointed people's court to pass judgment on their foes.

Eights must strive for innocence.

The well-adjusted Eights will find themselves shifting to be more vulnerable, needy, and open. They will start taking care of others in a much gentler way, focusing less on confrontation and more on cultivation. They can access their defense mechanisms from this standpoint in a safer, more productive way.

Type Nine Is the Peacemaker

- Triad: Defender

- Spiritual Focus: The agenda of others

- Weakness: Conflict

- Strength: Unconditional love

- Positive Direction: From being overly passive to the right action

- Essence: Universal love

- Secure Embodiment: The Performer

- Stress Embodiment: The Loyalist

- Wings: The Protector and the Perfectionist

Personality Case Example 1

Breanna is the assistant to the director of her mid-sized city's philharmonic orchestra. She is in charge of many aspects of the orchestra's production, from program design, to production management and to green room preparations. She also has a wonderful sense of musicality and is a violinist herself. She is thirty-one years old, and she is a loved figure in her community. Staff workers associated with the orchestra appreciate her warmth, her support, and her enthusiasm.

Breanna has a music room at home, and it is a mess. She has an assortment of old programs, sheet music, orchestra posters, and the room is dusty. She has some pieces of stage memorabilia here and there—a signed piece of sheet music from a famous cellist's folder is framed on the wall—and a cosmetically rough piano sits in the corner, piled high with stacks of papers. Music constantly spills from a speaker, the source of which is unknown. Breanna has a special place on her desk that is devoted to her husband and three small children.

Breanna makes it clear that she is casual and fun at work. She makes jokes, pokes fun at the players, and generally makes sure that they are having a good time with each other. To an outsider, her workplace looks extreme and chaotic, but it is controlled chaos. Breanna insists that she can't do her job without being chaotic in her office. She plays fast and loose with deadlines and rules, but she manages to handle responsibilities, albeit in a messy way.

She is aware of her issues with the organization. She tries sometimes to fix things up and keep them in order, but nothing ever seems to change. Sometimes, when Breanna gets overwhelmed, she might start blaming others when it is unreasonable. Eventually, Breanna got her own assistant and was able to bring more organization and order to her work and life.

Personality Case Example 2

Max is the director of a large non-profit that is based in Chicago. The organization coordinates funding for various programs that provide education to underserved populations. Max worked for years at a local university and rose through the ranks, becoming an assistant dean. Eventually, he started the non-profit with his friend and established it as a working organization.

Max is a single father to two children, one of which is now working after graduating from college. The other is about to leave home for school. Max and his wife split up years ago; she cited his passivity as one of the major factors for their troubles.

Max is an effective worker, and he is known as a great father. He also cares for people outside of his family. People know him as a person to whom they can tell their troubles. He goes to great lengths to help people. He is a good cook and enjoys being the guy people can rely on at a barbeque. Max tends to function by gaining energy from being around other people. People like to come to his home, which feels very comfortable. It is an interesting home, but you don't feel like you have to walk on eggshells there. There are a few pets around, all adopted from various shelters.

Max's business partner really values his support, and they work well together. He has learned when to give Max the lead and when he needs to fill in Max's weak spots on projects and coordination. Max has proven in his leading of the non-profit that he is an excellent mediator. When there is a discussion to be had with an administrator, donor, or other business entity, he is able to use his instincts to adapt his communication and create agreements. He makes people in the group feel that he is trying to get everybody together to benefit the whole community, rather than remaining stuck in petty or unnecessarily tedious issues. He has a warm, vulnerable disposition.

Max finds that he is mostly content in his life. He feels that if he sticks to what he knows, life will work out for the better. Things have gotten fairly stable and ordinary at this point, and Max is comfortable with that. However, Max sometimes finds that he feels lonely. He feels a little resentment that he does so much and does not feel that others do the same for him. Max does not like thinking about that, and he tunes it out by listening to a 70's rock 'n' roll record or watching a good movie.

The Peacemaker is driven by the need to avoid conflict. They have a gift of acceptance for others. They do not approach others with prejudice, and they make people felt understood and accepted. They can be very unbiased because they have a natural sense of kindness around malicious behavior. They express harsh truths very calmly and are able to handle matters of deep emotionality with power and grace.

It is arguable that the Peacemaker is a sort of default personality for humans, unaffected by the lack of skill or love from one's parents. If we had not grown up in whatever context we encountered early in life, we may all be Type Nines.

With all of their abilities for peace and kindness, the Peacemaker may have a hard time understanding their own needs and their own nature. They need to find out what they actually want, who they are, and how they can exist in the world.

Sometimes, the Peacemaker's problem is that they lack courage, or they do not have enough of a sense of self that they find themselves important enough to show their talents to other people. They can fade themselves in and out of everything and be everywhere but get nowhere. If something else broaches a subject, they take it up, though not necessarily with great passion. If their partner changes the subject, they address that. They like to swim with the current.

In childhood, the peacemaker may find that they were either overlooked or swamped. They were ignored or rejected if they expressed their own opinion. The interests of their family were more important than theirs. There is a collective bent to this personality type. Peacemakers may have found themselves as children in such a difficult situation that they had to find some reasonable middle ground. They may have learned to see both sides of a situation before they were truly mature enough to do so.

The Peacemaker is lovable. They are so charming and elastic. They like to take the path of least resistance and might be afraid of decisions that will pin them down into any specificity. The key vice of the Peacemaker is belittling themselves.

To ascend in his or her development, the Peacemaker must learn to access energy and drive to achieve goals. Nines benefit from gaining the ability to organize and engage. They often stay away from competitiveness or unrealistic expectations. The Peacemaker must remember that they themselves can enact change. When the Peacemaker is feeling depressed, they must remind themselves that inaction will feed their lack of motivation.

Chapter 3: Unlocking Interpretations

The teachings of G.I. Gurdjieff and Oscar Ichazo have much to do with the Enneagram gaining as much prominence as it has in recent decades. Ichazo and Gurdjieff were teaching far away from each other, using different methods and languages, but they had a common interest in helping people to become their deepest authentic selves through a program of inner work. Gurdjieff worked and lived in Russia and then France. Ichazo established a school in Arica, Chile in the 1960s, where he taught his way of using the Enneagram for self-analysis.

Gurdjieff connected a Platonic-inflected concept of essence versus form in his teachings. He taught that one had both essence and personality. The essence of a person is their nature; it is some inherent truth of their being. Our personality is what has arisen from the context and circumstances that we grow up and develop with from childhood. The way to finding one's essential self, to Gurdjieff, was spending time in a rigorous program of observing oneself, and that we all individually and collectively need to strive for transformation to evolve.

Oscar Ichazo is largely responsible for the Enneagram system of personality that most people work with today. Ichazo initially labeled the system of self-analysis used to work with the Enneagram as "proto-analysis." He had one particularly bright student named Claudio Naranjo. Naranjo studied with Ichazo, and he carried over Ichazo's teachings to Berkeley, California in the early 70s. Naranjo led groups of people participating in proto-analysis, and he taught about the personality types. Naranjo was born in Chile but trained in the United States as a psychiatrist. He took many different perspectives into consideration in his development and teachings, including Jungian archetypes, the work of Karen Horney, existential philosophy, psychoanalysis, and the work of G.I. Gurdjieff. The Enneagram struck him as a powerful tool for personal growth and an integrative model of personality.

The teachings of Gurdjieff, Ichazo, and Naranjo fall into several different categories of study. Some have suggested the term "psycho-spiritual," that is, addressing problems of both psychology and spirituality. When we compare the psycho-spiritual system of teachings presented by Gurdjieff, Ichazo, and Naranjo to psychoanalysis, we see a great number of similarities. Both theories of the Enneagram and psychoanalytic theory view personality as a result of the interaction of a child with the world. They both want to take into account the child's innate disposition and the child's environment. One difference is that psychoanalytic theory focuses a little more on childhood, and the Enneagram is applicable equally to children and adults.

There is a holistic quality to the Enneagram system of personality. It directs our attention to the tripartite division that we all experience in the head, the heart, and the body. This is mirrored in the intellect, emotion, and behavior. The Enneagram supports an equal consideration of body and mind, as often seen in non-western philosophy. The Enneagram supports a balance of these three for functioning.

When using the Enneagram to distinguish which Type you associate most closely to, you want to consider some different elements of the Enneagram's map of personality. The Enneagram makes some distinctions in categories: the gut, the heart, and the head types. These correlate to sexual drives, social drives, and self-preserving drives.

An important part of unlocking these personality types to better understand others and improve communication is recognizing that each person is a microcosm of the whole system. That is to say that all nine types think, feel, have a sex drive, a drive for self-perseveration, and social impulses. All nine types have strengths and faults. So, in parsing your own type and other personality types, you must remain conscious of the common attitudes that we have, and also the contextual factors for personality. Betty, in the office, may only be showing you one side of her that will lead you to think she's a Protector. But in most of her life, she is the Loyalist. When she is challenged to an extreme, she behaves like the Investigator. We may embody many different aspects of each of the personalities. If you were able to look closer into Betty's life, you'd see that she has core attitudes and developmental tendencies that align with the drives of one type.

What leads us to our most core personality type? People have to survive in the world! We start to organize traits and characteristics that will help us make our way and form relationships, with others and ourselves. Personality is made up of our defense mechanisms, habits of thought, the emotions that come with the thoughts, interpersonal aptitudes and abilities, and a way of physicality to manifest our energy. Once we understand our tendency to have one way of living, we can unlock the opportunity for proactive, rather than reactive behavior.

The Triads, wings, and variants of the Enneagram model can provide even further insight into our behaviors and tendencies. Both of the types on either side of any given Enneagram type are the wings of that type. People are never only one of the personalities described in the Enneagram; they are always a combination of one or two of them. This is one reason why no two people ever seem completely alike in their behavior. If an individual is mainly a Type Three, the wings of Type Three will also be present in their behavior and personality. This means that sometimes they may embody the characteristics of a Type Two, and sometimes they may imitate a Type Four. Some will say that an individual draws equally from both wings, that is, if they are a Type One, that they derive equal influence from each of their wings. Others think that people tend to characterize the influence from only one wing at a time.

Let us discuss the secure and stress embodiments of each of the types. The Enneagram's lines illustrate an individual's shift in personality when they are facing security, versus the shift in an individual's personality when they are feeling stressed or disintegrated. Each type has two lines that connect it to other points on the Enneagram. Depending on the type of situation that the person is facing, they tend to adopt or embody the characteristics of a certain other type. Here are the directions of the lines that illustrate the stress embodiment: One shifts to Four, Four shifts to Two, Two moves to Eight, Eight moves to Five, Five moves to Seven, and Seven moves to One. Within the triangle, Nine shifts to Six, Six shifts to Three, and Three shifts to Nine. When individuals are feeling safe and secure, and perceive themselves as healthy, there is the secure embodiment. The lines that illustrate the shift to a secure embodiment are such: One shifts to Seven, Seven moves to Five, Five moves to Eight, Eight shifts to Two, Two shifts to Four, and Four shifts to One. In the triangle, Nine moves to Three, Three shifts to Six, and Six shifts to Nine.

Wings of a personality certainly complicate things, but the geometry of the Enneagram is such that it holds a pattern and organization.

There are many different ways to look at the Enneagram. It may make sense to consider it a cycle in itself, starting from the Type One, moving to the Type Two, and down along the line. The Type Nine, the Peacemaker, is where the cycle restarts. The wings for a personality inform and affect the way that the personality is expressed. The Perfectionist, while having a huge drive for excellence, will sometimes find the need to help people as a "perfect" endeavor. This would demonstrate the Type One taking on the characteristics of its wing on that side. The Performer will sometimes find that they want to "perform" as a helper. This would be the Performer's wing of Type Two impacting them. Sometimes the Performer will have an artistic bent and will take up cello or painting or writing. It is no coincidence that the Performer is situated next to the Romantic, who is desperately in love with all forms of art.

Chapter 4: Identity and the Journey

If you haven't done so already, you may find it interesting to attempt a self-assessment of Enneagram type. You are probably the only one who can do this classifying for yourself; after all, you know yourself best. First, give yourself some time to study and look at each of the types, so that you can get a good picture of what each of them can look like. You may find a few different well-established Enneagram self-report questionnaires. One of them is the Wagner Enneagram Personality Style Scale. Another is the Riso-Hudson Enneagram Type Indicator. Before you take any type of personality inventory, you should make sure that it is coming from a trusted source and that it has sufficient levels of validity and reliability.

Most of the theories around the development of personality in the Enneagram acknowledge a humanistic viewpoint, influenced by the psychologist Carl Rogers, among others. Humanistic theory suggests that people come up with a set of defense mechanisms and coping strategies to maintain their safety and health in the world. Some of these coping strategies may be healthy, and some may not. This provides the distinction between adaptive coping strategies and maladaptive coping strategies. An adaptive coping strategy is a way that you deal with problems and challenges in the world that is healthy and helpful, without providing a lot of negative side effects. A moderate amount of exercise, expressing emotions through art, or attending therapy groups are examples of adaptive coping skills. Some examples of maladaptive coping skills would be avoidance (staying at home to avoid your problems), drug abuse, or violence.

Whatever coping skills we develop, that becomes a sort of identity in itself, and we start to think of ourselves as identified by those skills. In reality, these skills represent only a part of us, whether they are adaptive or maladaptive, and there is an authentic, ultimate version of us inside ourselves. The Enneagram presents a basic schema by which we can investigate our adaptive and maladaptive coping mechanisms. Often, the Enneagram can not only tell you about your faults but also how you are limiting yourself. You might hear a description in the Type that you realize you are not achieving because of some kind of block.

The Enneagram theory can be integrated with western theories of development quite well, and Claudio Naranjo did a lot of this in his work. Naranjo thought that in reaction to pain and anxiety, people seek to cope with an urgent situation with equally urgent coping mechanisms. When the urgent situation or threat is repeated, we find what works best, and we continue to carry out those behaviors. The behaviors become learned and rewarded and continued into adulthood.

This view is essentially congruent with the object relations theory. Object relations theorists believe that the personality comes out of the person's complicated way of adapting to his or her environment. The individual is striving for instinctual needs, such as the need for relationship. Another instinctual basic need is individuation or being different and sufficiently independent.

People, as we know, are extremely complicated. Obviously, nobody is perfect. There are many parents who meet their children's needs too little and some too much. As needs become unmet or over-gratified, the child develops coping mechanisms. If the situation stays the same for a long time, the behaviors will become fixed. This is what makes up our personality or character. A popular positive psychology adage goes, "Watch what you think, your thoughts become your actions. Watch what you do, your actions become your habits. Watch your habits, your habits become your character."

When this process is enacted negatively, it is almost impossible for a young person to analyze what has happened. The actions and habits become unconscious, and in this, the person becomes unconscious to the fall from consciousness. We start thinking that what we do is just who we are. This is often seen in addictions. The person starts to think, "I am Karen, I drink every night and that's just what I do." You can imagine all sorts of situations where people use this justification to continue with the negative manifestations of their personality. It ultimately results in the person being blocked from accessing their authentic self, and they may end up limiting their development into what they potentially could be.

Here's a more thorough description of how this happens:

> 1. Self-affirmation: This refers to the initial onset of the problem and the expression of need.
> 2. Negative environmental response: This represents the environment's (or parents') rejection of fulfilling that need.
> 3. The reaction: This is the automatic response to the rejection that has been experienced. It is often a negative emotional experience, ie, rage, terror, or sadness.
> 4. Self-negation: This step is where a child or person learns to turn against himself or herself. They are now trying to block the initial need that they expressed, learning that their needs cannot be met. They also begin blocking the experience of the negative environmental

response. It is an identification with the lacking environment. This is the onset of a potentially life-long conflict and is where many of our pathologies arise. It is where we learn how to keep ourselves safe by any measure, and often the measures become maladaptive.

5. Adjustment process: This can also be a lifelong process, wherein the person grows to learn how to compensate for the previous steps and to become more balanced and make compromises to resolve an unsolvable problem.

Therefore, we are left with our personality. The personality consists of which parts of you have expressed and which parts of you leave repressed. What we are dealing with here is suppression versus the exaggeration of our characteristics. With the Enneagram, we get nine descriptions of patterns of thinking, feeling, and acting that get in the way of our essential, authentic selves.

Let us go through the types and explore how the different vices and strengths of each can be caused by or accounted for by adaptive or maladaptive coping mechanisms. At the end of each description, a question is presented. This question may help each of the types to distinguish between their history of adaptive and maladaptive coping mechanisms.

Type One, the Perfectionist, is extremely ethical. They are guided by moralism and are often teachers or activists. They tend to have a deep fear of being evil or defective. Often the coping skills that the Perfectionist have developed will reflect their wish to be "good," and they may adopt very healthy coping mechanisms early on, such as eating well or exercise. However, there is the risk that the Perfectionist will struggle with setting a balance in these mechanisms and may struggle with eating disorders or over-exercising. On the other hand, the Perfectionist may sublimate their vice into dark corners that no one gets to hear about, which may involve substance abuse or other ways to blow off steam. When examining how your personality manifests, as a Perfectionist, you should ask yourself, "Why am I trying to be perfect? Who what or is telling me that I need to be perfect? Do I actually need to be perfect?"

The Type Two, or the Giver, is empathetic, genuine, and kind. They are often quite generous and love to help others. The Giver has a fear of being unwanted and not belonging anywhere. This is the drive to feel love. Givers will develop interpersonal ways to protect themselves in the world. They will use relationships to fuel their self-worth. They will often get involved in co-dependent relationships, in which they become dependent on others to be dependent on them. This is an example of a maladaptive coping strategy that the Giver will sometimes take. If the Giver were able to manifest their personality in a positive and healthy way, that adaptive coping skill would be that they develop intimacy early on, as they have a knack for doing. The Giver should be asking, "Am I sharing enough my weaknesses to the world? Am I allowing myself to be helped?"

Type Three, the Performer, is extremely goal-oriented, ambitious, and charismatic. They are excellent leaders and are driven by self-image and what they perceive others' images to be of them. The Performer was always driven, even at a young age, to do and achieve. This means that they learned early on to be successful and that that would be what keeps them safe and connected. Successes in school and work are certainly protective factors in the life of a child. However, these are the same kids who are pushed by their parents and tried to live up to unrealistic expectations. Resultantly, the kids often lose touch of what is important to them and find themselves lacking in self-awareness and contentedness. The Performer will find a strong dose of introspection will be helpful early in their journey. The Performer should ask, "Who am I trying to satisfy with my success? Am I truly feeling content with my achievements?"

Type Four is the Romantic. They are dramatic, love expression, creative, and can be self-absorbed. They are careful with their own intimacy but love diving into creative projects with depth. They are most afraid of not having anything significant about them, of not being unique. They want to establish their identity in the world and for people to listen to them. The Romantic often learned in early development that they had to find meaning for themselves; they found it hard to connect to what was around them and life felt dull. So, they set to work making things magical for themselves. And they usually succeed—even if it has costs along the way. In attending to their creative and artist-selves, they often reject or ignore the practical demands of living in the world. They may be very unorganized. The Romantic, as we know all too well from the biographies of many musicians, artists, and writers, may be predisposed to alcoholism or drug abuse, a maladaptive coping strategy. Their adaptive coping strategies include creating and participating in worlds of art or other esthetically fulfilling tasks. The Romantics should ask themselves, "Can I admit to myself that I have meaning? Can I admit that I am good and have inherent meaning as a human being?"

Type Five, the Investigator, is typically oriented to be alert and curious. They're able to find out why things are the way they are. They are always searching and always asking questions. The Type Five has a deep fear of being useless or incapable. They spend a lot of time looking, listening, seeing, and perceiving the world. The Investigator wants to be protected and empowered by knowing. This is all well and good, but sometimes, what we know can hurt us. The Investigator may have developed coping skills that included gathering information and knowledge to defend themselves from danger. They may have missed out on developing the adaptive skills of drawing boundaries and looking outside their limitations. The Investigator may want to ask of themselves, "How am I limiting myself? Can I accept that there are some things I will never know?"

Type Six, the Loyalist, is extremely committed in relationships and trusts friends more than anyone. They are very cautious and can be indecisive. The Loyalist wants to guarantee that they will never be abandoned. This is their basic fear—that their support system will up and leave them one day, without explanation. They can worry a whole lot. The Loyalists developed adaptive coping skills for maintaining relationships. They learned how to make friends with people and keep them as friends, by satisfying their needs or keeping them safe. The Type Six feels that if they have enough support, they will be okay. Type Sixes may learn maladaptive coping strategies that also stem from their type of relationality. They may find that they get into unbalanced relationships, perhaps on the other side of the Giver, and that they are needed only to fulfill the need of someone else. In this self-discovery process, the Loyalist should ask themselves, "Can I be okay with uncertainty? Can I acknowledge the impermanence of life?"

The Type Seven, or the Enthusiast, is always having fun, being spontaneous, and finding themselves with great versatility in social and other situations. They tend to be over-enthusiastic about the world, wanting to stay busy, and be fulfilled. They have a basic fear of being deprived or being in pain. Almost anything that catches the mind of a Seven will be accepted and taken enthusiastically. They often make the mistake of adopting an attitude of extreme idealism and become disappointed when the world doesn't live up to their expectations. Their idealism may have bolstered their adaptive coping strategies early on in life. Of course, why wouldn't someone want a friend who is always seeing the bright side and is always available to do that fun thing you planned. The other side of this is that they can get wrapped up in all of these ideas. They may find themselves keeping busy just so they can stay away from exploring their inner life, and they don't actually know what they want. Staying busy to avoid life is a common maladaptive coping strategy in our society. The Type Seven should ask, "What do I really care about? What am I rationalizing about that is not actually as awesome as I think?"

The Type Eight, or the Protector, is centered on power. They are assertive and strong. They use their resources well and are decisive. Their basic fear is of being harmed or controlled by others. They can also be known as the Challenger, as they love a challenge and interacting with others in a competitive way is a strong source of relationality for them. The adaptive coping strategies that the Protector learns to use are usually tied with assertiveness or aggressiveness. Perhaps more than other types, it is easy to see how this behavior can easily manifest in both adaptive or maladaptive coping skills. Of course, if the Protector is in a situation that is dangerous, they will be likely to defend themselves physically. There are other protective factors associated with assertiveness; they may learn to have their needs met more easily than less assertive types by being able to demand it. However, the path of assertiveness and the path of aggressiveness are often difficult to distinguish, and it can be difficult for the Protector to execute one without wading into another. The Protector should ask herself, "Is there a part of me that is deeply vulnerable?"

Type Nine is the Peacemaker. The Peacemaker is easygoing, affable, and trusting. They are often creative, can be enthusiastic, and helpful part of support systems. They have a deep fear of loss and separation. They want to have contentment in their souls and the souls of others. They are often "seekers" of spirituality and have a sense of connection to humanity as a whole, not just their particular cohort. The Peacemaker developed coping skills that are centered around making harmony in people and situations. This may have worked out very well for the Peacemaker. If the Peacemaker does not find himself or herself adjusted well as an adult, however, they might find themselves often just "going with the flow," on one side of a codependent relationship, or just not having their needs met. Their maladaptive strategies may involve being the "yes man" or an enabler. This is where they have found protection. However, as the Peacemaker develops, they learn to have an integrated self, which delineates their own needs as well as the general need for harmony. The Type Nine should ask, "What do I really want for myself that might mean others do not fully approve of my choice? Am I missing out on something important to me because I am afraid to disappoint someone else?"

The idea of life as a journey is one that permeates all of our historic archetypes and pervades our mythology, literature, and art. Thinking of life as a journey can be helpful in accepting context. Our context is where we are, what we are, how we are, and when we are. For some, the Enneagram is a topic with which they are well familiar. Some people have engaged in self-discovery and analysis for decades before coming across the Enneagram. Where are you in the journey? Whether you are young or old, no matter what resources you have, you are on the journey. This journey, however, is a paradoxical one. There is no beginning and no end. To be striving to find that day where the journey has an end is a mistake; this has been found in historic Buddhist philosophy. Each day has its challenges and successes, from the first to the last.

If you use the Enneagram to gain insight into your life, you are giving yourself the gift of understanding. To gain understanding is an essential part of being human. Understanding where you are in your journey is important. Be kind to yourself. The voices of judgment may come strongly in some minds, but the Enneagram is an egalitarian system of categorization. There are no hierarchies, there is no personality that is better than another, and the beginner is just as valid as the guru.

Indeed, we must see the key vice in our personality not only as an evil thing to be avoided and controlled but rather one to be harnessed and used for good. There is a certain "dissociative" response to vice. We have extreme feelings of shame, guilt, or punishment that reinforce our avoidance of the vices and negative tendencies in our personality. The thing is, our vices have a lot to teach us about ourselves. They tell us about how we defend ourselves, how we relate to others, and how we see the world. The Enneagram invites you into a dialogue with your more negative parts and helps you to see them as part of the whole you. Your creative exploration of the

Enneagram should be filled with encouragement and a thirst to become a responsible and whole person.

The Enneagram can be great for multiple people to work on together in small groups. If you are able to find this kind of support system in your Enneagram work, then that is great. Having a small group of people allows you to talk about what you are finding out about yourself and feel safe to explore the shadowed sides of our personality. Sometimes, others might see you in a different light than you are able to see yourself. They can point out things they have noticed that correlate to Enneagram knowledge, or they can help to clarify your thinking.

Once we can interpret the Enneagram and unlock the meanings of the various personalities and how to interact with them, we are often left with the question of how we go forward and work with the knowledge that we now have. There are many answers to this question. Some of them involve personal dives into the depths of your inner self and allowing introspection as the catalyst for an agent of change. This will be easier for some than others, and certainly, some will get lost in the depths of their own souls. Introspection can sometimes lead a person to the next step of their development. This can be seen in behavioral changes, such as a young adult who decides to settle their life for the first time. It may be very intertwined with artistic pursuits such as music, visual art, or writing. The journey toward change and self-realization may involve seeing a counselor, religious leader, or family elder for consultation. There is a huge variety of styles of counseling available, from CBT (cognitive behavioral therapy) to hypnotherapists and everything in between.

Whatever the case is for the path taken for change, we now have enough understanding of the brain and its neuroplasticity to know that adaptation in individuals is totally realistic and possible. Neuroplasticity is the brain's ability to create a new connection and grow more cells in response to experiences. This ability to grow and adapt at the neuro-psychological level includes both connections that help us to live healthier and have better relationships and connections that don't. This is where awareness can help us. Self-awareness is understanding our thoughts and feelings and being able to see when we are displaying features of a certain type, for better or worse. The Enneagram can help us to use labels and make sense of our personalities so that we can see our tendencies, and when appropriate, act differently! The Enneagram paradigm allows for deeper understanding, and ultimately, self-acceptance.

The Enneagram is a cosmic symbol, and as such, has different forms and functions. Its geometry is situated in a universally harmonious way, and the geometry of the Enneagram contains a way to map interrelationships that are found in human tendencies and behaviors. One way to use the Enneagram as a map in another way is an Enneagram for a process of transformation.

The following list is a contextualization of the Enneagram. This one uses the outer circle to describe the temporal events and the inner triangle to denote the phases of inner and outer self-development. Here's how this one is set up:

1. Clarify the Problem
2. Plan Initial Strategy and Gather Resources
3. The Value of the Problem Enters
4. Conduct Initial Work to Solve the Problem
5. Find a Way to Solve the Problem
6. Vision of Solution Enters
7. Work Out the Details
8. Present the Results
9. Process Completed/Problem Enters

The outside of the circle illustrates the functional aspects of transformation. It is what goes on during the cognitive tasks we complete regarding problems. Point 0 is when the problem enters our consciousness. We feel attracted to the problem and want to solve it. This is also the feeling of our previous problems leaving. The circular nature of this problem represents the circular nature of having problems in the first place!

Point 1 is the task of clarifying the problem. This does not always prove to be as easy as it may appear. What exactly and precisely is the problem? Sometimes, the problem gets blown out of proportion or minimized. Let's say that John wants to be more emotionally available. His problem is that he is not sufficiently emotionally available. Or is it? While participating in the type of introspection that is necessary to come across this problem, John may look closer at his problem and realize that he doesn't feel that he personally has enough emotional support. This, rather than the first problem, may become the more important or urgent problem.

Point 2 is to plan and gather. "What are you going to do about that?" This step is a great challenge for some people. For those who suffer from indecisiveness, which can stem from depression, sometimes this is as far as they get. Just try not to decide that you can't do anything about it because that is not actually true.

Point 3 is the value of the problem. Sometimes, we need to choose our battles. Sometimes, the time and effort it takes to solve a problem may necessitate a surrender of sorts. In John's case, realizing that he needs a greater emotional support system, that is a very important problem. It is a problem that, if worked on, will provide the individual with many rewards.

Point 4 presents the initial work that is needed to solve a problem. This phase of transformation will be easier if the first few steps are completed successfully. If you are able to make this a straightforward task, it will be easier to complete. Our example case, John, may take this time to start working on establishing connections he has lost, or opening up to others in a mild, moderate way, to get things started.

Point 5 is where one must find a way to solve the problem. This can be a stage of great tension, especially if the problem is producing enough stress that a threshold for change is met. This stage contains magical moments. John may discover that someone else feels the same way he does because he put in the work and went to a social event, or he may find he has more courage because of a new connection. This is where we get oriented to the solution.

Point 6 is the vision of the solution. It enters the consciousness and allows us to complete the process of solving the problem. Typically, we start to "get it." In this stage, John is realizing the behaviors that will unlock better social support and is getting better at doing so.

Point 7 is to point out the details of the solution. What is actually needed to see this thing through? This is where the solution becomes solidified, rather than one that happens instantly, the solution manifests itself over time.

Point 8 presents the results or puts the solution in a form that connects with you. This is to acknowledge that you put in the work to achieve a transformation in your life and put it together so that you can repeat the helpful steps in the future and improve upon your process.

The concepts of awareness, communication, and understanding are all needed to navigate this process successfully. If you don't get caught up in all the emotional and behavioral blocks, these steps can provide a method to responsible deal with difficult situations.

Chapter 5: Types and Communication

Communication is a very oft-cited problem in relationships. In many different developmental phases, people can find themselves with a low level of self-awareness. The Enneagram can help us increase levels of self-awareness and understanding. It is with this self-awareness and understanding that we can begin to build healthier, better relationships, ones marked by clear and open communication. What gets passed on in this communication is our needs, our goals, and our vision for our lives. The typology of the Enneagram can help us to realize how we are acting and gain insight into our behavior and relationships.

When faced with a struggle of interpersonal dynamics, we can often get caught in a reactive feedback loop. The problem presents: a person becomes annoying or too needy.

Here is an example case of how an awareness of your own and others' types can lead to a more harmonious work environment.

Katherine works as a full-time university professor, teaching English in multiple classes for college undergraduates. Katherine is a Perfectionist, an Enneagram Type One, and she believes that her strong sense of justice, along with her high expectations and strict standards, have bolstered her ability to be successful in her field. She has recently taken on Sam, a new associate professor, who will be taking on some of the instruction in her classes. Sam is the Enthusiast, an Enneagram Type Seven. Sam took on a great deal of preparation and brought in lesson plans for a month in advance when he started. Katherine was greatly impressed by this, as it shows a high level of expectations and organization. Their initial meeting left them both feeling great about their new work relationship and excited to be working together. They got along quite well, although sometimes Katherine finds that Sam is a little more high-energy and sillier in the work environment than she would be. At first, she interprets this silliness as enthusiasm and sees that Sam is eager to learn and be liked and improve in his work, which she can understand.

As the weeks go on, however, Katherine notices that Sam is starting to sway from staying on track in his classes. He is very smart and competent but often strays into tangential subjects that get too far away from the class material. Sam has also begun to reschedule their weekly supervision meeting. Katherine has consistently marked in her calendar a day and time to meet, and she wants to stick to that time consistently. Sam reschedules the meeting a couple of times, and Katherine brings up that she wants to have the meeting at the originally scheduled time. Katherine points out that it was their agreement to meet at this time every week. Sam agrees but also interjects that they are still meeting every week, just not at that time. "That is not the point," she thinks.

Sam begins to show up at the originally scheduled time for the meeting, and this continues for a few weeks. Then Sam attempts to reschedule the meeting, and Katherine becomes angry, bringing up that it is unprofessional to reschedule meetings at such a high frequency. Sam lets her know that he is very busy and has several projects that he is trying to maintain outside of this job. Katherine dismisses this point outright. Sam walks out of the office feeling misunderstood and bemoaning Katherine's rigidity.

Katherine wonders what to do. She ponders various answers to the situation and then remembers training in which the Enneagram was used to facilitate understanding of students. She realizes this could be a situation that could greatly benefit from some understanding. She sends Sam the assessment tool for the Enneagram and asks him to bring it to their next meeting.

When Katherine and Sam meet, they discuss that Sam is the Enthusiast, and to feel happy, he sometimes needs to feel like he is busy. He enjoys teaching, and he has the gift for it but has trouble having the trust in himself to make major commitments like this one requires. He feels that by diving completely into this job as an associate professor, he is missing out on some other opportunities that he might have. He is active in volunteering work, giving some of his time to a local non-profit that works with underserved populations. He is part of a softball team, takes violin lessons, and works out every day. All of these activities have left him feeling tired but fulfilled, and he is exhausted nearly all the time. This is his reason for missing supervision meetings. His intention is not to be disrespectful or unprofessional, but he can't bring himself to drop any of the other treasured activities. He recognizes, with Katherine in the room, that his spontaneity can sometimes come off as impulsivity and unprofessionalism.

Katherine, the Perfectionist, an Enneagram Type One, tells Sam that she understands that she can be perfectionistic and rigid sometimes, especially when she feels that she is not being respected. She shares with Sam that she has a deep desire to educate, share her wisdom, and help young people live better lives. She knows that she can be bossy and critical, but it comes from good intentions, the intention of wanting to help others reach their potential. She tells Sam that it is difficult for her sometimes to loosen up and be flexible. She also recognizes the emotions that it brings up in her when people around her do not demonstrate the same adherence to structure.

The two of them sit down and have this conversation, and in the end, they are able to see what each of them needs individually and needs to provide for the other. It is important that Katherine has enough structure to be able to facilitate the type of work environment that she needs. Sam needs some flexibility in scheduling. They work out a system for when he needs to reschedule; he will let Katherine know enough in advance so that it doesn't affect her weekly schedule. They both agree that they will engage in open communication about their needs and obligations. Katherine will try to provide equal amounts of positive feedback and criticism for Sam's teaching. Sam will create a lesson plan at least a week in advance to be approved by Katherine.

They leave this meeting both feeling understood, connected, and settled with each other. Neither of them tried to change their personality to fit the situation; they both acknowledged aspects of their personality and accepted that they are two different people working together. What they have done is provide insight into their situations. Katherine gained some insight about what her personality does to people. Sam gained some insight into how his life can work better for the people around him. They are establishing a relationship of safety, trust, understanding, and connection.

Katherine and Sam experienced a conflict of personality dynamics in their relationship.

If you examine what happened here, you will find a pretty good set of characteristics for the "intervention," or whatever needs to happen to make a relationship functional again.

One of these is acceptance. There are many people in the world who find in themselves an ability to judge and then compartmentalize. What does this mean? It means that they have parts of themselves that they have not accepted. It may be an experience that was not able to be integrated well into their understanding. It could be a bad choice they made years ago which affected their life. It could be circumstances outside of their control which they can't accept.

For example, let us take the Type Five, the Observer. The Observer is that smart kid who sits in class and never talks, although you know that he knows most of the answers that the teacher is asking the class. He thinks of the answer but doesn't say it out loud. Early in childhood, this mostly works; adults can perceive the level of intelligence that these children often have, and they can tell that the child is this type. However, as we develop into young adulthood, we are expected more and more to represent ourselves through our speech and to develop verbal communication in order to be part of the group and develop relationships. There may be a teacher that comes along and says to that kid, "You did very well on your written assignments and tests, but I can't give you an A, because you never spoke up once during times of class participation." The Observer will then have to accept this point: their natural tendency has, thus far, worked, but that they have come to a time when this underdeveloped aspect of their personality must be bolstered and used more. The way to communicate with a Type Five in this situation is like this: you give them a reason. You can say, "You're going to have to learn to express yourself, make yourself seen and heard. You have good ideas, and you have smart thoughts about the material. I would love to see you speaking up more." Acknowledge that his abilities are not undervalued.

Let us explore more aspects of Katherine and Sam's way of coming together and communicating using the Enneagram to guide the way. Another thing that they are employing is awareness. Awareness, simply put, is noticing what you are feeling, seeing, hearing, thinking, or doing. Both Katherine and Sam had a level of awareness. Katherine probably has a higher level of awareness, due to her years of experience versus Sam's youth. Katherine was able to use her higher level of awareness to notice her thoughts, feelings, and actions. At first, she noticed that she felt upset when Sam would miss a meeting. She was able to recognize her feelings and later explored her feelings, to see what the root cause might be. There are different levels of awareness, and the first level is knowing what you experience in the here-and-now. When you feel the physical sensations of fear (e.g., the tightening of the chest or pounding of the heart), you cognitively label it as fear. Recognition is the first step, and you will be surprised to notice that it can be very difficult for some people. People have to learn how to identify and label emotions. Oftentimes, children will have trouble labeling their emotions and will say that they feel "mixed up" or not have words at all to describe how they are feeling. Adults have this problem as well; someone might think of their agitated state as anger, when in fact what they are feeling is fear and panic. Once a person can use this first level of awareness to notice and label emotional experiences, they can find deeper meaning and the underlying causes of the emotional experiences. Maybe it was not anger that you felt when that person cut you off, but maybe it was an intense sense of fear because you had an experience in a car accident. Sometimes when you are yelling at that customer service representative on the phone, you are not really yelling at them. You're yelling at your mother, your childhood teacher, or your uncle.

At a higher level of awareness, we are sorting these things out—why did I feel that anger yesterday? Was I able to express it appropriately? How was I presenting my anger? Did I keep it inside? Oftentimes, there are deep, unresolved issues that we find when we really pay attention to the emotions and thoughts that are happening throughout our experiences.

In Katherine and Sam's case, Katherine used her sharp skills of self-awareness to reassess her situation. She knows that she dislikes when people are late and realizes that there might be another side to the story. When Sam consistently was missing meetings, another, less-self-aware version of Katherine might have kept that feeling built up until they felt like they had no choice but to fire Sam. Katherine stayed cool, however, noticed her anger and frustration and decided to do something about it. What did she do? She initiated a responsible, two-sided conversation about who she is and who Sam is. Sam had at least enough awareness to know that he desires to stay busy but also wants his position working with Katherine. However, if Katherine wasn't able to take the initiative to ask him to explore himself, he may have never gotten there. Once Katherine and Sam were able to establish and identify their personalities, they each saw a side of the story that they could not see before. They each have separate drives, some conflicting and some congruent, and they both have needs, again, some conflicting and some congruent. All of these drives and needs are valid. They just needed to identify the problem and communicate with each other about it.

Let us discuss some of the pitfalls that people run into when they are trying to communicate with people. The first is lack of clarity. When you talk to someone about interpersonal issues, or really, anything, it is important to say what you mean and mean what you say. If you would like to tell May that her music is distracting to you, try not to say, "May, that music sucks." You might think that you are making it clear that you want the music to be turned down a little bit, but you are not. Such a response would just mock her taste, when she may not even know that her actions are affecting you. Obviously, it can sometimes be difficult to make yourself clear, especially if the subject matter is difficult to discuss. On the other hand, sometimes you may need to amplify your concerns. If a Type Two, the Giver, is presented with a problem of a person obstructing their own needs or desires, they can sometimes tone down their needs or ignore them altogether. Rather than, "Hey, do you think you could consider not doing that?" try, "That's not working for me," or "I need to find a solution for this problem." Clarifying your thoughts can do wonders for communication.

Another important aspect of communication is kindness. This can be harder for some types than it is for others. The Perfectionist is a classic example; they can sometimes have trouble keeping their criticisms of others constructive and may have a binary view of what is good. They tend to use this judgment on themselves and it leaks out into their judgments of other people.

Now, you may find that you are not always in the type of situation that will allow for a sit-down conversation with somebody about each of your personality types. Of course, every tense interaction we have in a month cannot possibly lead to a meeting similar to Katherine and Sam's, because that is obviously impractical. However, by taking some time to consider why you are the way you are (a cogent way of describing what the Enneagram can do for you), you will be able to at least grow an understanding of yourself. From there, the world tends to open up to people. You can use your understanding of yourself to find the capacity to understand others.

For example, let's say that you run into a book about the Enneagram of personality. You read it, start to get interested, and immediately recognize yourself as Type Six, the Loyalist. You read a little more and start to see yourself in a different light. You start to read about the other types, and you have more analytic thoughts. Some of the characteristics in the other types match you as well, and you find yourself labeling your family members and coworkers. This helps to spark a new pattern of awareness around different types of people. You might find that the vigilance you keep is something that you now understand in a different light. This new awareness can serve as a framework for thinking about other people. When there is a difficult or tense situation, you can have a little bit of perspective on what makes you the way you are, and how another person might be experiencing you.

Another thing to consider when using the Enneagram to improve communication is to analyze the communication styles of the different types. Each type has strengths and weaknesses in their communication style. Type One, the Perfectionist, tends to be honest and polite. They might run into trouble, however, when they drift toward their natural tendency to use words that evoke judgment in their communication. A Perfectionist should strive to remember that others do not necessarily ascribe to their standards and expectations, Ones can try not to say that people ought to or should do things the way they perceive matters should be done. They can be very opinionated. One tip for the Perfectionist to try is to tune into your body language and pay attention to what the body is saying.

Type Two, the Giver, will be able to listen very well. They are generally good at asking questions, as they enjoy eliciting the feelings and thoughts of others. Type Twos find themselves at home in many relationships and communicates well with certain types. The Giver should try not give too much-unsolicited advice, which they can sometimes preoccupy them. The Giver often needs to work on expressing their own feelings, whatever that looks like for them. By being more honest and in the moment with their communication, the Giver can maintain clearer boundaries.

Type Three, the Performer, is often very confident, and this helps their communication. They are good at communicating regarding problems and good at finding solutions. It will often be an enjoyable experience to talk to a Type Three. They can become impatient, sometimes, with overly long conversations or emotional conversations. The Type Three Performer often needs to learn to listen to others more. This can be achieved by learning about active listening—asking questions, making eye contact, and showing an interest in a person's conversational interests.

Type Four, the Romantic, can hold conversations that are very deep and intense. They may mirror the Giver in this regard. A Romantic's communication is often non-judgmental and non-superficial, making them adept at finding a person's meaning. Sometimes, they can be too intense, searching for some deeper meaning where there isn't any. One tip for a Four in his or her communication is to remember that you can't have an incredibly deep connection with everyone; it's just not possible.

Type Five, the Investigator, is good at being respectful in their speech. They usually can find something to amuse them, and they like to observe others in their speech and communication patterns. The Five, like the Two, is often lacking in their ability to share of themselves with their own feelings, so a tip for Fives in their communication is to share more personal information and feelings with others and to try not to worry about what others will do with that information.

Type Sixes, the Loyalists, like to have complex conversations. They will enjoy a serious topic, and they will be able to have a sense of humor about serious things. They tend to be witty and ironic in their speech. They might become overly reactive in some situations and should strive to be less defensive and more responsive. A Type Six should look to become less questioning of other's motives and trust their own insight.

Type Seven, or the Enthusiast, likes to tell long stories. When you are trying to follow the logic of a Seven, try to remain open and focused, as it can be easy to lose them. They are light-hearted and talk quickly. They are good at engaging people and keeping them interested in their stories and jokes. A Type Seven might find that they need to tell a few less stories and ask others more questions to improve their communication.

Type Eight, or the Protector, is often very direct and candid. They can use their bluntness for good or bad outcomes. They like action and are interested in confronting others and being confronted. The Eight can be a little demanding in their speech, which is something to look to improve over time. They can also be dismissive and become angry more easily than some other types. A Protector should try to listen to those who they don't hold in a high regard. They might find that they have misjudged the person.

The Type Nine, or the Peacemaker, is generally relaxing to interact with for others. They are generally good communicators and like to affirm others. They establish rapport easily and make friends well. Sometimes, the Nine will have a low expression of themselves, or they might be ambiguous and indecisive. A tip for Nines to improve their communication is to be honest and open and share their thoughts more quickly with others.

Chapter 6: Understanding Self, Other, and Triads

There is no point where anyone, perhaps save a few monks and spiritual ascetics who claim to have reached enlightenment, who gets to the end of personal development and can say, "Now I'm perfect." The key to working with ourselves is to establish a dialogue with ourselves and with our development. This does not mean casting judgment upon ourselves but that we must pay attention to our thoughts, habits, attitudes, and needs. Understanding is part of awareness, and the more understanding we have of the journey of our life so far, the more we can understand how to deal with problems and improve ourselves.

Some psychology theory will be presented here to clarify some of the more complex parts of the Enneagram structure. The character issues and themes in the Enneagram present a system of development in the inner triangle of the symbol. There have been many theories of development in spiritual and psychological studies, and the Enneagram is congruent with many of them. The inner triangle connects Type Nine, the Peacemaker; Type Three, the

Achiever; and Type Six, the Loyalist. Each of the points also categorizes the nearest two types into the same category, creating three groups of three. These are known as triads. They break down into three previously discussed concepts—the body, the head, and the heart. This mirrors the developmental tasks that we must face in our youth according to the psychologist Margaret Mahler. Mahler's system included the phases of differentiation, practicing (or exploring and testing for danger in the world) and rapprochement or negotiating one's own need for individuality with the need to have relationships.

A person can go through these stages quickly and all at once in childhood, or it may be stretched out long into adulthood. They may also be cyclical stages, gone through time and time again as a person enters new developmental phases of life. You can see that Mahler's developmental issues match up nicely with the Enneagram's inner triangle. The "body" types are mostly oriented to the merging that people experience. They have difficulty with differentiating themselves. These types of people may find that they take on the feelings or attitudes of other people too much in childhood.

Points Two, Three, and Four are the emotional or heart triad; points Five, Six, and Seven are the mental or head triad; and points Eight, Nine, and One are the instinctual or body-based triad. The emotional triad is called Attacher, the mental triad is called Detachers, and the instinctual triad is called Defenders.

The Defenders (instinctual or body, anger or differentiation triad)—Types Eight, Nine, and One are Defenders. They are self-protected; they fight against others or at least move against them when necessary, as a way of making sense of and operating in the world. The Defenders will find that major tasks of development in their lives center around differentiation and independence. Each three of these body-based types will express their search for differentiation in different ways. They will experience conflicts and patterns related to self-definition, and this is the struggle that underlies the core developmental journey for each of these types. Now, the search for differentiation or becoming aware that you have the power to be independent and considering yourself worthy of independence is a part of everyone's journey. For the Defenders, however, this task remains an issue that they will most always be dealing with in some fashion. This distinguishes them from the other types.

Sometimes our path to differentiation will come and go smoothly, and other times it will not. For the Defenders, this will affect the development of their identity and personality. This is a basic human struggle that is mirrored in our births. Before birth, we are one with another person physically; we live inside that physical body and that is natural and good. The defenders may have a hard time getting over the spiritual trauma of having to leave that state, entering the cold and indeterminate world. We can imagine the infant's perspective at this developmental stage. Part of our development as humans is becoming physically able to live. We must separate from the perfectly symbiotic physical fusion of the womb. If you look at the types extending around the circle of the Enneagram, you can see the process of transformation from totally merged, into becoming more independent and self-referencing.

As infants experience the initial phase of life, they all have to deal with this problem. As a baby develops in the very first months, they have a gradually increased awareness of themselves as a separate human being. The mother's reaction to this process is very important. The mother also experiences this separation, and the optimal situation is that the mother processes this experience and is able to support the baby and also support the child's natural move toward differentiation. Everybody is human and makes mistakes, so it is easy to see how mothers may not always provide the perfect balance of affection and support for autonomy.

This is where many of the Defenders, or Body Triad types, may have experienced a problem. There may have been interruptions to this process, or they may have experienced it as highly tumultuous. For example, if there was a lack of structure early in life, the Type One, the Perfectionist, may try to compensate for this by establishing extreme measures of organization and standards to the highest level later in life. Type Nine, the Peacemaker, may experience this stage as a block, and never feel like they completely differentiated from their initial environment. The Peacemaker is often someone to which we can all relate; it represents the essential experience of all humans to a certain degree. Type Eights, or the Protector, may indicate a lack of holding in their personality. They became tough to protect themselves because no one else was protecting them.

The Attachers (emotional or heart, sadness, or practicing triad)—Type Twos, Threes, and Fours—are outer-directed, moving toward people, striving to make sense of and operating the connection to people and relationships. One thing that most Attachers have in common is a defining characteristic that comes from childhood fear. This has to do with separation anxiety.

This stage of development is associated with moving away from differentiation and toward the "practicing" phase, which is the process in which a child goes out into the world to test it and see how dangerous it is. You could think about a toddler, who loves to explore the world. The toddler, no longer limited to the visual perspective of crawling or lying down, has a brand-new vision of the unknown world. This is the phase of practicing physical tasks that are needed for independence, like walking or other daily activities. There is often a delight that the child experiences in the external world. This can come with some narcissistic tendencies, as to be expected in early childhood.

Some Attachers say that they had an early experience that was very startling to them during this phase. It may have caused them to retreat back into themselves or to a place of safety. Attachers may not experience an ongoing sense of fear, but they have an underlying motivation for their behaviors that stems from a desire to avoid fear. This developmental stage can certainly provide a sense of overwhelming bewilderment at the world. If you can imagine a child's consciousness at this point, you can imagine how wild the world must seem. A significant part of the practicing phase centers on the individual's experience of their parent as an individual person, rather than a part of them.

These issues are deeply held in the consciousness and subconscious of Attachers. The tension here is between the need to adapt and achieve in a new realm of existence and the need to keep an important relationship. The awareness of this tension grows in the toddler. Then, the child wishes that they could share every new experience and skill with the parent. The child will be looking to the mother to have a sense of validation during this phase so that the child knows that the mother sees them and approves of their newfound autonomy. Attachers, or Heart types, will feel unlovable and "broken," if they are not shown the sufficient amount of emotional support and mirroring during this phase. Type Threes that are in this situation will find the strategy of achieving to be lovable. Type Twos will find that they tend toward the strategy of giving and adapting to others. Type Fours will strive to be unique, creative, and artistic to earn love.

The Detachers (mental, head, fear, or practicing triad)—Type Fives, Sixes, and Sevens—are inner-directed. They move away from people; they detach as a way of making sense of and operating in the world from inside one's head. This stage of development is associated with moving away from the practicing phase and toward the "rapprochement" phase, which is the process showing a child has accomplished certain measures of independence, such as being able to walk, but their desire for independence becomes affected by their fear of abandonment. The child, at the beginning of their physical independence, always comes back to the mother. They feel exuberant to come back and share with the parent what they have done in the world. At some point, the child will learn of their limitations; they might run into a particularly intimidating experience that limits their ability to continue. They then have a dilemma between their independence and the proximity to the caretaker. The way that this stage is negotiated successfully is when the caretaker is able to provide sufficient "scaffolding" to support their child in their explorations without the child becoming preoccupied with anxiety.

Some Detachers note that they had a difficult experience at this age. It may have caused them to retreat back into themselves or to a place of safety. Detachers have a sense of safety within themselves, rather than wanting to depend on others for their security. The Detacher has a specific tendency to want to use their inner life to maintain a sense of self, rather than externalizing or depending on others.

The tension from this stage of development is focused on abandonment. The child whose parents mistook their caution in this stage as weak or ineffectual may have instilled deeply troubling fear of abandonment in the child. It grows a discomfort with new relationships, and the Detacher will always be wondering if their friends or romantic interests will leave them spontaneously.

People make their way in the world as Attachers, Detachers, or Defenders. Now that we have looked at some of the developmental aspects of the triads, let's discuss how the traits of each of the triads manifest in adulthood.

Type Eight, the Protector, is in the Defender triad. The Protector lives with an intense sense of power. The Protector's way of living in the world is by confrontation. This comes from early experiences where confrontation was necessary, even forced upon them, and it helps them to make sense of what matters and what they can do. They deal with the lack of control they had as a small child by wanting to exert their control as an adult. The Protector may have a pessimistic view of the world and move through the world in a suspicious way. They use confrontation as a way of connection. That guy giving you a hard time about going the wrong way in the parking garage? That might be his way of talking to a stranger today. This may serve a purpose for him, whereas you are just annoyed. They can feel when someone is not being honest because they get scared and want to protect themselves. They like to empower people with challenge and support.

Type Nine, the Peacekeeper, is also part of the Defender Triad. The Peacekeeper likes to focus on the harmonious aspects of life. They like to try to create peace all over, from the workplace to the convenience store. They are easy leaders, but they don't enjoy conflict. This is where they differ from the Protector. The Protector likes to confront others for connection. The Peacekeeper likes to mediate others for connection. They are good at being friendly and laid-back not only with friends and family but also in professional relationships. They are relatively non-competitive, and they believe in the concept of a level playing field.

The Peacekeeper has trouble initiating action, however, and if we compare that to Mahler's first stage, we could postulate that they do this because they are afraid of conflict. Conflict, in early life, was something they had to take on unsupported, and the Peacemaker wants to avoid that. They take on others pressing demands and they rarely express anger. Some Peacemakers may need to do some self-work to be able to express their own anger.

Type One, the Perfectionist, is the third of the Defender triad. Their inner voices and life are focused on achieving and seeking perfection. They have a deep sense of what's right. They think that they know how to fix most problems. They often feel that they owe it to themselves to be the most competent. Think about the associations we have with the parents of perfectionists. Often, just like their children, they have the desire for everything to be perfect and will often push their children into achieving roles. The Perfectionist, then, developed their achieving self, and maybe forgot to develop the self that is just okay, and needs affection.

They can be good leaders and inspire others to reach great heights as well but must watch to make sure they do not continue a cycle of forced-perfectionism, as this can be very damaging.

Another aspect of childhood development that is notable with Perfectionists is their severe inner critic, which tells them that they have to constantly be perfect and that doing something for enjoyment isn't productive. They can have a devastating sense of failure when faced with something they are not able to do. This comes from early messaging from the parent. They may be mirroring a parent's behavior, or they could be just reacting to very high expectations from their environment. Time is the enemy of the Perfectionist because they feel that they will never have enough time to complete all they need to do.

Let's move to the Attacher Triad. The main mode of being is emotional for those in the Attacher Triad. The types included here are Two, the Giver; Three, the Performer; and Four, the Romantic.

Type Two, the Giver, is in the Attacher Triad. They struggle to know their own needs. They have trouble with differentiation. The Giver is very sensitive to what is going on with other people. They are motivated by others' needs. They are often very good at conveying warmth, knowingness, and understanding because they do have a genuine concern for people. They sometimes get frustrated because they are not able to do as much as they would like. They get into codependent relationships and can be obsessive.

We can see how Mahler's second stage of differentiation has influenced the Giver's personality. The stage with which the Giver has become preoccupied is the first one, where an infant is just beginning to understand the difference between "me" and "you." The Giver just wants to live in symbiosis forever, with them being able to help people, and to a certain extent, keep them dependent. Perhaps this is a reenactment of the unhealthy relationship from which this attitude derived, in early childhood, putting themselves in the parents' place.

The Giver will develop an environment where they can help people and get into the type of relationships that give them energy. The well-adjusted Giver will find ways to have their own needs taken care of as well.

Type Three, the Performer, loves to perform; it is as simple as that. Simply and bluntly put, they do this for attention. This is not meant as a reduction of the value of the Performer's pursuits; after all, the Performer often achieves incredible heights in many ways throughout their life. They like to think of themselves as role models. They usually have an excess of confidence, efficiency, and skillfulness. They bask in the applause and approval that they get from achieving.

The last of the Attacher Triad is the Romantic, or Type Four. The Romantic has a sense of uniqueness, and they are very comfortable in their idiosyncrasies. They think of themselves as different from others, and sometimes this can lead to loneliness and suffering. They feel that they have a gift that is theirs. They care deeply about people and look for meaning in life.

You can see how the task of differentiation affects each personality type differently, although, each of the Attachers is striving to deal with the primal nature of differentiation, they try to get there in different ways. As for the Romantic, it is enough for them to establish that they are different and unique, and unlike anything else in the world. This soothes their tension of having to be differentiated from others and helps them think of themselves as people who are worthy of meaning.

The Romantic usually embodies emotionality and drama in their life. Their relationships often take on a dramatic tone. They are relational people; they regard themselves as the type of people who are good at relationships.

The issues that the Romantic often experiences in childhood can lead to issues with boundaries in adulthood. The Romantic may get caught up in the feelings of others. They may catastrophize and are very inconsistent in relationships. They have a cycle of expectation and romanticization that always gets undercut by reality.

The final Triad that we will discuss is the Detacher Triad. The Detachers include Type Five, the Investigator; Type Six, the Loyalist; and Type Seven, the Enthusiast.

The Investigator, or Type Five, will often find that they move away from people. They want to detach from the world and realize their thoughts and emotion in their inner life. This makes them feel secure. They minimize participation as a way of keeping themselves safe. This is involved with Mahler's second stage of development, the practicing stage. This is when a child is experimenting with how far they can venture out of safety and still come back to it. The Investigator will always be trying to find answers and make connections in their own mind. They look for extreme approaches to problem-solving. They like to look at the world as a puzzle. Each piece might be separate, but together, it creates an understandable whole.

In early development, the Investigator may have had issues in the practicing stage. They may have experienced themselves as separate from the parent in this stage, and they realized that perception would be what keeps them feeling good. Perception will safeguard from the difficulties in life. This may be a function of feeling distant from the parents as a young age.

The Investigator is objective and often stone-faced in serious conversations. They like to consider all different points of view and label them all valid. They are very cautious with their time and energy and can be very good at anticipating the demands of a particular job or task.

The next of the Detachers that we will talk about is Type Six, the Loyalist. The Type Six has some of the most easily drawn lines to childhood experience. The Type Six regards the world as dangerous and unsafe. They will find that their experience often lines up with a pursuit of safety from their perceived threats from the world. They are very good at locking into what is dangerous. They do not like to confront, and they do not like to escape. They are very loyal and will often be very good friends. They do not care much about being in positions of leadership. They alternate between being rigid and lax.

The task of Mahler's second stage is autonomy. Autonomy is being separate from the other. At this stage, they are developing a sense of differentiation. The Loyalist might find that at this stage; they may have had problems finding the safety outside of the immediate connection of the mother, and this will affect their ability to find independence and a healthy sense of self as an adult. They experience time as something to obey.

The Enthusiast, or Type Seven, is very optimistic. They love to think about the world and the future, developing exciting plans. They sometimes have to experience the harsh sense of reality and may escape into their inner world where they are not limited.

They dislike doing the same thing twice. They like newness and freshness. They derive energy from stimuli from multiple sources and direction.

They like to plan and think about possibilities. They will stay late up at night thinking about their next month, how they will travel, or make their world more exciting.

The Enthusiast has a great sense of self. Enthusiast who has not adjusted well to adult life may find themselves with a sense of entitlement. They may come across as believing that they are entitled to the pleasant life of their dreams. This can be shown through a lack of empathy for other people, placing their needs before others.

What is shown in the Enthusiast's maladaptive coping skills is a failure to have a sense of self or a lacking in self-concept? This comes from the developmental phase of autonomy that has been previously mentioned.

One meta-perspective on the Enneagram and how we fit into the world is an analysis of the type of personality who thrives in our context (for now, we will be talking about North America, particularly the U.S.). It is all about productivity. This attentional focus emphasizes getting things done, producing, and winning. The strengths of this group include efficiency, reliability, self-confidence, leading, and goal orientation. However, there are many weaknesses that come along with this productivity and winningness. Type Threes tend to brush aside feelings, be impatient, manipulate facts, be deceitful, and believe their own lies. They will detach from soft feelings and demand everyone to be productive.

When we participate in a culture, we perpetuate its collective myth. The ethos of a country can be identified by looking at the attitudes and ideas refinement in its art, mead, traditions, government, and economy.

One way that this is observed is in the expectations of the gender roles. Our culture tends to value two opposing but symbiotic values: will and love. The women grow up expected to be mothers and lovers, and culture will often tell them that these are the values that should shape what they do for work and in their personal life. Love in this binary system represents empathy; it is the value of being able to relate to a person, understand them, and make them feel like you understand them. The tools that one needs in order to have conveyed this includes being a good listener, being humble, giving of yourself, and being unegotistical. This is obviously a positive and incredibly valuable set of traits, but sometimes these traits are developed at the expense of other traits.

The opposing but symbiotic trait of "will" is assertiveness. Men are told that this is what they must develop at all costs. They must be able to defend themselves, to be leaders, to dominate physically. Sometimes, they are told that they must learn to dominate psychologically. The tools that you need to develop for this include confidence, a sense of self, and strength. You can see how the development of these traits could engender the under-development of other traits more closely related to love.

When you are examining your personality type, and the ways your personality get trapped or is successful, it is important to consider this binary spectrum for yourself as well. You can ask, "How much love am I able to show? How much will I be able to enact?" When examining these, you might compare them to the expectations of your gender, and this can help illuminate aspects of your personality that are difficult to see at first. A rebellious young girl may focus more on her assertive side because she notices that the world wants her to be a certain way, and she loves going against the grain. This could be the manifestation of a variety of types, for example, this could fit in with the Protector, the Performer, or the Individualist. Likewise, a young man might find that he severely lacks the qualities of assertiveness and dominance and that he finds the way he moves in the world is closer to a feminine perspective. A Type Four Romantic can often be this case or a Giver. Understanding the role that expectations from society play in our development is crucial to giving yourself some context. Context helps us to sort all this stuff out.

Conclusion

Thank you for making it through to the end of *Enneagram: An Essential Guide to Unlocking the 9 Personality Types to Increase Your Self-Awareness and Understand Other Personalities So You Can Build Better Relationships and Improve Communication*, let's hope it was informative and able to provide you with all of the tools you need to achieve your goals whatever they may be.

The next step is to put into action some of the concepts and awareness that you've developed through the process of reading this book.

Finally, if you found this book useful in any way, a review on Amazon is always appreciated!

Check out more books by Matt Holden and Kimberly Moon

Manufactured by Amazon.ca
Bolton, ON